The Holy Spirit in Action

The Holy Spirit in Action

The Person and Work of the Holy Spirit

Compiled by

Homer G. Rhea

Pathway
PRESS

Library of Congress Catalog Card Number: 96-070140
ISBN: 0871484196

Copyright © 1996 by Pathway Press
Cleveland, Tennessee 37320-2250
All Rights Reserved
Printed in the United States of America

Contents

INTRODUCTION
By Marcus V. Hand

Israel began observing the Feast of Pentecost after reaching the Promised Land, but the instruction for the celebration was given while they were still in the wilderness. The Old Testament festival mandated that worshipers go to their priests on the 50th day after Passover, carrying basketfuls of "firstfruits" held high, or elevated. Each worshiper was to proclaim loudly: "I declare today to the Lord your God that I have come to the land the Lord swore to our forefathers to give us" (Deuteronomy 26:3, *NIV*). On the Day of Pentecost they were to acknowledge that God had fulfilled His promise to them. Pentecost was to declare to God and to everyone around them that they had entered into the Promised Land!

Pentecost in the New Testament issued the same proclamation. The outpouring of the Holy Spirit in Acts 2 acknowledged that God had fulfilled His promise (Joel 2:28, 29). Through the Pentecostal experience, believers today declare that in Jesus they have entered into the blessing that the Promised Land foreshadowed. In Christ we are complete. In Him we have the fulfillment of all the promises of the Bible. In Him we are free to experience all the good gifts God gives to humanity.

Of all the gifts God gives us, one of the most important is the gift of the Holy Spirit. This Gift is not some theoretical idea or philosophical teaching. The Holy Spirit is a person; He is God.

In Pentecostal worship, we proclaim that in Christ we dwell in the place where the promises are fulfilled. We have received eternal life. We have received the promise of the Father, the Holy Spirit (Luke 24:49). We haven't received all His promises yet—we haven't "arrived"—but we have entered into the "land of promise." The Holy Spirit is at work in us!

The purpose of this book is twofold:

1. **To enrich your spiritual life by acquainting you with a Biblical perspective of the Holy Spirit at work.** This is done through the study of Scripture passages, using with them up-to-date, real-life illustrations. It is hoped that the reading of this book will enrich your spiritual life and help you know Jesus Christ better. Our aim is to enhance your devotional life.

One cannot read the Bible and not be struck by the magnitude of the Spirit's work. The record of His activities in Biblical times illustrate His nurturing care. Further, one cannot view the move of God across the contemporary scene without knowing that the Holy Spirit is working still.

2. **To enrich your spiritual life with teaching on the Holy Spirit and give you a guide which will, hopefully, motivate you to walk daily in the power of the Spirit.** The experience of Pentecost is still a valid experience. Hundreds receive the Holy Spirit every day. The promise of the gift of the Spirit is made to all whom the Lord calls (Acts 2:39). The prayer of the writers of this material is that you will allow the Holy Spirit to work through you.

This book is composed of 13 chapters, each by a different writer. The gifts of the Spirit, the fruit of the Spirit, worship, discipleship, and many other topics are covered here. Several elements make the material easy to study and teach.

- *Introductory page.* An introductory page appears at the beginning of each chapter, containing a thought-provoking idea or question that leads the reader into the heart of the teaching. This page may be reproduced and used as an overhead transparency or as a handout sheet.

- *Questions.* Questions are placed at the conclusion of each chapter to provoke thought and discussion. Meditating on what you have read and discussing these matters with your group reinforces learning, and it helps you to remember.

- *Learning activities.* Learning activities are placed at the conclusion of each chapter which help to reenforce the teaching all week.

- *Lesson outlines.* A section in the back contains a teaching outline for each chapter. These will be valuable aids as you teach these lessons to your study group. Permission is granted to reproduce them for use as overhead transparencies or as handouts.

This series of studies on the Holy Spirit may be taught on family night or on Bible study night. Elders may teach them to the believers under their charge and study leaders may use them for women's Bible study. They are inspiring to read and will enrich your personal devotions as well.

"In the last days, God says, I will pour out my Spirit on all people" (Acts 2:17, *NIV*).

We have received the Holy Spirit. We have come to that "last days" point in history the Bible tells about. The Holy Spirit is being poured out today in an unprecedented way. Let us celebrate as Pentecostal believers and declare loudly that God has fulfilled His promise of sending the Holy Spirit.

We have entered the place of fullness in Christ—the "land of promise."

Chapter 1

NAMES OF THE HOLY SPIRIT

Make a list and discuss the meaning of all the names of the Holy Spirit you can think of.

_____

_____

_____

_____

NAMES OF THE HOLY SPIRIT

by
J. Anthony Lombard

Scripture: John 14:16

INTRODUCTION

The Church of God Declaration of Faith states, "We believe in one God eternally existing in three persons; namely, the Father, Son, and Holy Ghost." The Father is a person; the Son is a person; the Holy Spirit is a person. Scripture reveals that each is a distinct personality, has a distinct function, and is known by a variety of names. Names for God include *Elohim*, "Almighty"; *Adonai*, "Master"; *El Shaddai*, "All-Powerful"; *Yahweh*, "Jehovah"; and *Jehovah-Jireh*, "Provider." Names for Jesus include Son of God, Son of Man, Redeemer, Immanuel, Christ, Lord, and Messiah.

Names for the Holy Spirit include Spirit of Grace, Spirit of Life, Spirit of Adoption, and Comforter. The *New King James Version* translates *Comforter*, in John 14:16, as "Helper." This message looks at some of the names of the Holy Spirit which reveal fresh dimensions of His earthly activities.

SPIRIT OF GRACE (Hebrews 10:29)

From Adam to Christ, sin reigned! Until Jesus came, all mankind lived in fear and in bondage to death. Death, unknown until Adam sinned, became mankind's most formidable foe. Therefore, death became Satan's most lethal weapon against God's creation. Too strong to defeat and too cunning to outsmart, Satan enslaved all humanity in the bonds of what appeared to be a hopeless future. But then . . . the Spirit of Grace came calling!

The Spirit of Grace reveals love's initiative. *Grace*, a rich and powerful word, projects a mental image of one deserving punishment for wrongdoing but, instead, is forgiven. The person is forgiven, not because of innocence, but because the One offended is gracious in love and forgiveness. After the crucifixion, resurrection, and ascension of Jesus, the Father sent the Holy Spirit in response to the prayer of Jesus. The Holy Spirit's descent was love's provision for unredeemed humankind.

To Jews who lived under constraint of the law, the presence of the Holy Spirit was a refreshing spiritual release. To pagan Gentiles who had not known divine love, the Spirit of Grace was freedom from sin's dark rule. To Jew and Gentile alike, this was a moment of spiritual revelation and release. For the first time, they understood what was meant by the statement "If the Son makes you free, you shall be free indeed" (John 8:36, *NKJV*).

The Spirit of Grace reveals love's supremacy. The manner in which the Spirit of Grace came to earth at Pentecost (Acts 2) was a divine statement. A new day had arrived! The Spirit of Grace came to call sinners to salvation and break Satan's dominion for all who respond to God's love. The name *Spirit of Grace* displays the superiority of the Spirit's ministry in relation to the weakness of the law. The test is no longer legal obedience as the basis for salvation, but faith in the blood of Christ as the way to God. "But as many as received him, to them gave he power to become the sons of God, even to them that believe on his name" (John 1:12).

The law *demanded* righteousness of man, whereas grace *gives* righteousness to man (Romans 3:21, 22, 24). The law is connected to Moses and works; grace is connected to Christ and faith (John 1:17). The law blesses the obedient; grace saves the disobedient (Ephesians 2:8). The law demanded that blessings be earned; grace is a free gift of the Spirit. The law was an instructor teaching about God; the Spirit of Grace is *God in us, the hope of glory* (see Colossians 1:27).

The Spirit of Grace is God's most eloquent statement of His love for sinners. The Holy Spirit graciously offers Jesus as the sole remedy for sin. Good intentions cannot break sin's grip. Good works cannot erase sin's stain. No system of human merit, no religious rite of human ingenuity, and no sacrificial offering can suffice for sin. The Holy Spirit graciously offers Jesus as the only way to God. "For if we sin wilfully after that we have received the knowledge of the truth, there remaineth no more sacrifice for sins" (Hebrews 10: 26).

The Spirit of Grace expresses God's love. It is no trivial matter to receive the Spirit's call to redeeming grace. God does not take our resistance to His overtures lightly. To highlight the seriousness of rejecting Jesus as our sin sacrifice, the writer of Hebrews described it as doing "despite unto the Spirit of grace" (10:29). He reminded his readers of the severe penalty imposed upon anyone who receives the knowledge of the truth and continues in willful sin (v. 26). The writer of Hebrews indicated further that rejecting the Spirit of Grace is a heinous offense. To ignore Jesus, as not only a remedy for sin but the only remedy, invites an ominous response from God: "Of how much sorer punishment, suppose ye, shall he be thought worthy, who hath trodden under foot the Son of God, and hath counted the blood of the covenant, wherewith he was sanctified, an unholy thing, and hath done despite unto the Spirit of grace?" (v. 29). To treat Jesus as common is to deny His sonship. To reject Jesus as Savior is arrogant disdain for His sinless sacrifice. Such acts insult the Spirit of Grace. No deeper wound can be inflicted on the heart of God than to refuse His only begotten Son, whom the Spirit of Grace offers as a sin sacrifice.

SPIRIT OF LIFE (Romans 8:2)

God created Adam and Eve and breathed into them the breath of life . . . and they became living souls (Genesis 2:7). The breath of God that infused life into mankind was the work of the Holy Spirit, the Spirit of Life. The character of life for all creation and for all times was radically changed in that one act. The Spirit's work showed there is life for all, but eternal life is for mankind alone. In the Garden of Eden, God walked and talked daily with Adam and Eve in visitational intimacy. It was this relationship of intimate fellowship that Lucifer, who became the devil, lost and envied.

The Spirit of Life deals with mankind in sin. With deception, the devil deceived Eve and she sinned. Eve influenced Adam, and he sinned. Adam and Eve, in broken fellowship, were driven from the Garden of Life into the darkness of spiritual death. The Spirit of Life, the eternal character of creation, was withdrawn as a universal blessing and narrowed to the confines of the Garden in Eden. Under a curse, the earth's once productive soil became stubborn and stingy. Flowering fruitfulness battled to survive the choking invasion of weeds and thorns in an environment profaned by sin and under curse from God. The Spirit of Life withdrew from universal fellowship to sporadic appearances and individualized disclosures to a select domain. In the pain of broken fellowship, Adam heard the Spirit of Grace calling, offering hope for mankind hopelessly lost in spiritual darkness.

In Genesis 3:15, God canceled death's future! "And I will put enmity between thee and the [seed of] woman, and between thy seed and her seed; it shall bruise thy head, and thou shalt bruise his heel." This terse declaration sent shock waves through Satan's domain. In this utterance, God delivered the first gospel message. It was good news to Adam and Eve standing in shadows outside the Garden of Eden . It was good news to a world experiencing the pangs of disease and decay. This was good news to generations yet to be born into the fallen human family. Jesus came to cancel death's rule. What was lost in Eden would be restored just outside Jerusalem.

The Spirit of Life deals with believers in hope. Jesus is God's answer for sin. He came to "destroy the works of the devil" (1 John 3:8), including mankind's bondage to spiritual death. When Jesus, the seed of woman, died, Satan "bruised" His heel. But when Jesus arose from the dead, He "bruised" the head of the "serpent." Jesus manifested and demonstrated the power of the Spirit of Life. Shortly before His ascension into heaven, Jesus promised the Holy Spirit, who is the Spirit of Life, as a residing Presence. By this act, Jesus established a "new rulership"—"the law of the Spirit of Life" (Romans 8:2). Pentecost marks the beginning of the superintendency of the Spirit of Life as a universal, empowering, and residential presence.

Jesus died outside Jerusalem, and 50 days later the Holy Spirit descended inside Jerusalem, establishing a new rulership for those freed from the bondage imposed by sin. Under the law of Moses, sin was exposed; but it never rescinded control. Through the Spirit of Life, there is now freedom from sin's oppressive rule and hopeless future. For the first time since Eden, sin's victims were liberated from the power of sin and death. Through the Spirit of Life, sin's rule could be broken, sin's stain removed, and sin's curse lifted. The Spirit of Grace calls sinners to God, and by the Spirit of Life those who hear and repent are born again! The Spirit of Life establishes a rulership of love—imputing a new relationship, instilling a new pursuit, and releasing a new power!

SPIRIT OF ADOPTION (Romans 8:15)

Adoption has to do with identity. The word *adoption* is a family term. Its social usage gives clear meaning to its spiritual use. Therefore, this is the first truth that rises out of a study of this word.

In Galatians 4:4-7, Paul described what adoption means: "But when the fulness of the time was come, God sent forth his Son, made of a woman, made under the law, to redeem them that were under the law, that we might receive the adoption of sons. And because ye are sons, God hath sent forth the Spirit of his Son into your hearts, crying, Abba, Father. Wherefore thou art no more a servant, but a son; and if a son, then an heir of God through Christ."

Adoption is a legal act by which one is placed into a family, given the adopting family's name, and made an official beneficiary of all that the family owns. The adopted one may have been orphaned because of death, desertion, abuse, or rejection. But as an adopted family member, the adoptee shares the privileges, joys, and intimacy of the adoptive family. By the Spirit of Adoption, those once estranged by sin can now rightfully call God "Abba, my very own dear Father."

Adam's sin made the whole human family spiritual orphans. Rebellion and sin separated from God those created after His likeness and in His image. Everyone who confesses sin and accepts Jesus as Savior is "born again" by the Spirit of Life. On the basis of this spiritual birth, believers who were once spiritually orphaned are brought back into the family of

God by the Spirit of Adoption. They are not only rescued from sin, they are reinstated to full family privileges in the family of God. They can speak as a son, live as a son, and enjoy the privileges of a son.

The apostle Paul declared that the event which establishes our adoption beyond doubt is "the redemption of our body" (Romans 8:23). A number of supernatural acts, some immediate and some future, validate our adoption into the family of God. We, who were strangers and aliens from the commonwealth of grace, are now sons and daughters of God.

But there is more. The crowning act which validates our adoption is what takes place when we receive our full inheritance. Our bodies that were once "sold under sin" (Romans 7:14) will be changed and made "like unto his glorious body" (Philippians 3:21). The natural body, now subject to disease and death, will be made a spiritual body. We will be given eternal residence in the Father's house (John 14:3).

Adoption has to do with authority. Those adopted now have the privilege to call themselves "sons of God" and to function in the authority of sons. The Spirit of Adoption gives them the authority to do so. Everyone does not have this right. Even demons recognize the unauthorized use of the name of Jesus (Acts 19:13-17). It is presumptuous and unacceptable for anyone not legally adopted to claim sonship. An adopted one has the right to speak in the authority of Jesus' name. There is power in the name of Jesus, but only to those whom the Spirit has adopted into God's family.

Adoption has to do with privileges. There are wonderful privileges for those whom the Spirit adopts into God's family. Family members have freedom of access to God. Family members do not have to ask permission to eat at the family table. Family members do not have to make reservations to spend the night in the family home. The Holy Spirit gives immediate and direct access to full family privileges to all who are adopted into the family of God.

By the Spirit of Adoption, members of the family of God are empowered with the keys to the Kingdom: "And I will give unto thee the keys of the kingdom of heaven: and whatsoever thou shalt bind on earth shall be bound in heaven: and whatsoever thou shalt loose on earth shalt be loosed in heaven" (Matthew 16:19). As authorized "key holders," those adopted by the Spirit have authority to use the family name. Those once barred from entry into God's presence because of rebellion and evil are now given free and continuing access into His presence. Those once restricted from the inner family circle are now permitted free movement into its fellowship and intimacy. Those once "foreigners and strangers" now participate fully and freely in family plans and privileges.

Adoption has to do with inheritance. "The Spirit itself beareth witness with our spirit, that we are the children of God: and if children, then heirs; heirs of God, and joint-heirs with Christ" (Romans 8:16, 17). A sinner adopted into the family of God is granted the same legal rights in the family inheritance as a biological child. The Spirit of Adoption recognizes members of the family of God as legal heirs of God. Those whom the Spirit adopts stand to inherit equally with Jesus, demonstrating the full rights of sonship. Adoption accomplished by the Spirit guarantees full family recognition and reward. The Spirit of Grace calls us, the Spirit of Life transforms us, and the Spirit of Adoption affirms us full family status as an heir of God.

THE COMFORTER (John 14:16, 17)

Jesus is God's clearest disclosure of Himself to fallen humanity. His brief life on earth exposed God's love in rare splendor. After His death and resurrection, Jesus prepared His disciples for His departure from earth. He assured them of two things: first, He would provide them the abiding presence of the Holy Spirit as Comforter; second, He would give them exclusive revelation of truth through the Holy Spirit. "And I will pray the Father, and he shall give you another Comforter, that he may abide with you for ever" (John 14:16). This promise assured the disciples of the same care by the Holy Spirit that they had received from Jesus.

The name *Comforter*, as it relates to the person and work of the Holy Spirit, has both a specific meaning and a broad meaning. The Greek term from which it is derived was commonly used in the court of justice. It described one whose specific responsibility was to serve as legal counsel or advocate for a plaintiff. In a broader sense, the term describes one called alongside to provide assistance or to guide.

Jesus said the Spirit would give believers the same kind of ministry in His personal absence that He had provided in His personal residence. The ministry of the Holy Spirit as Comforter is an "omnipresent" ministry. He will be with all of us, at the same time, wherever we are. In this sense Jesus said, "Verily, verily, I say unto you, He that believeth on me, the works that I do shall he do also; and greater works than these shall he do; because I go unto my Father" (John 14:12). As One who resides in individual believers, the Comforter enables believers to accomplish works greater in number than did Jesus. The Holy Spirit as Comforter multiplies the works of believers by His omnipresent residence in believers.

To understand the Holy Spirit as Comforter, we must go beyond mere sentimentalism. The Holy Spirit as Comforter promises God's abiding presence, validates the person and work of Jesus as Savior, initiates a new era of Spirit-life, and provides valuable insight into the present and the future.

John's Gospel presents four distinct insights relating to the Holy Spirit as Comforter.

The Holy Spirit's ministry as Comforter is the same as that of Jesus' in *kind*, but different in *duration* (John 14:16). By praying for the Father to send "another" Comforter, Jesus meant that the ministry of the coming Comforter would be the same as that of the Father and the Son. The coming of the Comforter is the final manifestation of the cooperative work of the Trinity in bringing salvation to the world. The Comforter provides Christ's power and presence to believers in the personal absence of Jesus.

While the Comforter has come with the same ministry as the Father and the Son, the physical duration of His ministry will "abide forever." The Father loved the world and gave; the Son loved the world and saved; the Comforter loved the world and stayed. The work of the Father and the Son was *for us*, but the work of the Comforter is *in us*. The Comforter is to the believer what Jesus was to the 12 apostles. In this sense we can say, "He has never been away."

The Comforter gives validating witness of Jesus (John 15:26). It is little wonder that the Day of Pentecost was such a display of power and glory. Through the ages the Holy Spirit had been waiting for the day when He would come and energize the redeemed to war against the powers of Satan. When He descended from the Father, He came in a gusty, blazing, ecstatic manifestation. He did not come as a lazy breeze, but as a tornadic storm. This startling manifestation of the Spirit revealed the nature of the Father. He is awesome in His power and unsurpassed in His glory. The Comforter did not come to be a silent idea, but an empowering residential presence. No believer needs to be victimized by Satan's deceptive schemes. The Comforter came from the Father to restrain Satan, to condemn sin, to supernaturally empower believers for bold witness, and to guide believers in a daily walk in divine truth.

The Comforter has but one mission and that is to testify of Jesus. How does He testify? By empowering those who have been saved by the blood of Jesus to do the same things Jesus did. Only those supernaturally empowered can do the things Jesus did. The Comforter raises human ability to the level of the supernatural; and in doing so, He testifies to the sovereign power of Jesus to deliver sinners from Satan's bondage. The Comforter comes from the Father and manifests the Son through ordinary people by signs, wonders, and miracles. It is this supernatural manifestation that arrests the attention of unbelievers and attests the truth that Jesus is Son of God and Savior of sinners. The Comforter delivers sinners from Satan's evil rule and empowers believers for spiritual warfare.

The Comforter's earthly ministry could not begin until Jesus' earthly ministry ended (John 16:7). Jesus' departure from earth was not to escape conflict with the devil. He left because he had completed His divine mission and He was preparing the way for the Comforter to come. Jesus said, "If I go not away, the Comforter will not come unto you." Imagine how eagerly the Comforter must have waited to be deployed to earth to empower believers. He could not come in His fullness until Jesus had completed His mission. So deep was their respect for the other and so unified was their mission that neither person of the Trinity would hinder the work of the other.

This unity of purpose should be a lesson to all who are involved in the work of God. It calls us to love one another, respect one another, and make room for one another as we minister in giftedness and fulfill our calling. So unselfish was the Father's love that He gave His only Son to die for our sins. So unselfish was the Son's love that He gave Himself as a sin sacrifice. So unselfish was the Comforter's love that He waited for Jesus' departure from earth to descend in blazing power to equip the church to take the gospel to the unsaved of the earth. The Comforter's abiding, energizing presence assures us that our faith is not in vain.

The Comforter will amplify truth and announce things to come (John 16:13). Years ago I heard someone say of another, "They don't lie, but at times they do leave out some mighty important facts." We live in a world rampant with religious deception. How does one know whom to believe and whom to worship? Every major religion claims its own savior and its own bible. How do we know which to believe? The Comforter serves as a truth-guide amid the maze of deceptive religious teachings in our world. John said, "He will guide you into all truth." This implies that truth may not always be discovered at once. Truth begins with fundamentals and builds on this foundation. This is the way we learn conceptually.

And this is the way God informs us about things of the Spirit. The Comforter helps us sort through all the information we have to discover and discern the truth. This is a spiritual process, not an intellectual exercise. Truth is the only antidote for untruth. Divine revelation is God's cure for deception. In fact, the unspiritual mind cannot conceive the things of the Spirit. Therefore, the Comforter can only lead those who have been spiritually renewed into the knowledge of supernatural things. It is reassuring to know that the Comforter has come to guide us into truth and to guard us against spiritual error.

The Comforter provides revelational knowledge understood in progressive amplification. Note 1 Peter 1:10-12:

> Of which salvation the prophets have inquired and searched diligently, who prophesied of the grace that should come unto you: searching what, or what manner of time the Spirit of Christ which was in them did signify, when it testified beforehand the sufferings of Christ, and the glory that should follow. Unto whom it was revealed, that not unto themselves, but unto us they did minister the things, which are now reported unto you by them that have preached the gospel unto you with the Holy Ghost sent down from heaven; which things the angels desire to look into.

Prophets who foretold events far in advance of their times did not understand the full implication of their prophecies. Even angels desire to "look into"—to see with spiritual understanding—the things which the Holy Spirit, the Comforter, reveals. The Comforter provides us with knowledge that is hidden from those who spoke it—even from angels who do God's bidding (1 Peter 1:12).

Little wonder that we should rejoice and be glad as the Comforter unfolds before and within us the mysteries of heaven!

CONCLUSION

The person and work of the Holy Spirit did not originate at Pentecost (Acts 2). The Holy Spirit's work began with Creation and continues today. We are privileged to view the Holy Spirit's ministry from a historical vantage point. History becomes a witness as the Holy Spirit testifies to us through His mighty acts. More than a witness, however, the Holy Spirit is an inner presence energizing and guiding us day by day. He speaks truth and gives comfort. He reveals Jesus, and He reveals events to come.

For this invaluable ministry, we pray, "Come, Holy Spirit, I need You."

QUESTIONS

For Thought:

1. Meditate on the names of God listed in the opening paragraph. Think what each means to you.
2. The Holy Spirit is the "Spirit of Life" in you. How does this make you feel about your life?
3. What does it mean to you personally to know that you have been adopted by the Spirit into the family of God?
4. Rehearse to God and give thanks in your personal devotions for some of the ways the Holy Spirit makes a difference in your life.

For Discussion:

1. Discuss the meaning of "Spirit of grace" in conjunction with God's righteousness in us.
2. What is the meaning of each of the four implications of spiritual adoption? Discuss each one.
3. Jesus comforted; and He sent the Holy Spirit as a Comforter. Talk about the similiarities and differences.

ACTIVITIES

1. Often, names reveal something of a person's character or personality. Research the meaning of your name and find out if it is representative of you personally.

2. Now ask the Holy Spirit, the Comforter, to direct you to someone who needs comforting. Allow the Holy Spirit to use you as an instrument in bringing consolation and hope to that individual.

Chapter 2

THE HOLY SPIRIT IN THE OLD TESTAMENT

Name and discuss three ways the Holy Spirit may be termed "pro-active."

THE HOLY SPIRIT IN THE OLD TESTAMENT

by
Reginald W. Spooner

Scripture: Genesis 1:2

INTRODUCTION

The Holy Spirit is introduced in the Scriptures before the first two verses of Genesis are completed. The second verse tells us much about this third person of the Trinity.

Two Hebrew words in Genesis 1:2 help us understand the personality of the Holy Spirit—*ruwach* and *rachaph*. *Ruwach* is variously translated "spirit" (but only of a rational being), "breath" (exhaled forcefully), and "wind." *Rachaph* is translated "to move," "to flutter," "to hover," "to brood." These words reveal some basic truths about the Holy Spirit.

The Holy Spirit moves. He is Deity in motion! When we picture the Father, we see Him high and lifted up on a throne. We think of Jesus, the eternal Word, at His right hand. When we think of the Holy Spirit, we have difficulty picturing Him because He is pure spirit and a moving force. Yet, He is as much a person as the Father or the Son.

Without implying weakness or inadequacy, I would like to call the Holy Spirit "the Restless One." He is constantly moving.

THE SPIRIT MOVED IN CREATION

A characteristic of the Holy Spirit revealed in Genesis 1:2 is found in the Hebrew word *rachaph*. One of its meanings is "to brood." He is like a brooding hen jealously guarding her eggs. The earth had become without form, empty, and dark. Some scholars believe judgment had fallen on the earth sometime in the dateless past between Genesis 1:1 and 1:2. The Hebrew word *tohuw* translated "without form," also means "desolate, empty." This same word is used in Isaiah 45:18, where it is translated "vain": "God himself that formed the earth and made it; he hath established it, he created it not in vain, he formed it to be inhabited." This could be understood to mean that God did not create it thus in the beginning but that it had become "without form and void" (*was* can also be translated "had become").

Some believe that Genesis 1:1, 2 suggests a time lapse between these two verses. If so, something happened to bring the darkness and chaos. It would have been, then, over this judged and punished earth that the Holy Spirit brooded, bringing about the divine commission: "Let there be light" (v. 3).

The Holy Spirit still moves today to bring deliverance to man who is "condemned already, because he hath not believed in the name of the only begotten Son of God" (John 3:18). In the Old Testament, the Spirit strove with man before the Flood. The awesome declaration was given: "My spirit shall not always strive with man" (Genesis 6:3). After that, the floodwaters of judgment came. He has not changed. He strives today before the terrible judgment of the Apocalypse shall fall. His Father heart still yearns for every "prodigal son." He still calls to all who need to be renewed. He still broods. God still responds, "Let there be light."

THE SPIRIT MOVED IN HUMANITY

God rested on the seventh day of Creation; but after man sinned, we find the Spirit in action, striving with man. He who was so prominent in Creation is now active to bring about re-creation—a "renewing of the Holy Ghost" (Titus 3:5). He moves, and He moves upon man. There is a forcefulness about Him. Even when *ruwach* is translated "breath," it connotes a forceful exhalation. Genesis 6:3 reveals that the Spirit strives with man. The Hebrew word for *strive* means "to contend, to plead the cause (as at law)." Genesis 4:26 says man began "to call upon the name of the Lord." Enoch and Noah responded to this forcefulness, this striving, by becoming great men of God.

The Spirit is sometimes expressed in Scripture as wind. Jesus, in talking to Nicodemus, used that terminology (John 3:8). On the Day of Pentecost, there was a sound from heaven like a rushing, mighty wind that filled all the house (Acts 2:2).

Our family lived for a while on the high plains of Kansas. The wind blows there almost constantly. Not only was it nearly constant, but at times it also seemed all-pervasive. My wife often found little piles of sand which the wind pushed in through the closed windows. The wind invaded my plans; it reminded me of its presence when I was driving. I stopped trying to take the family on picnics. The phrase "the winds come sweepin' o'er the plains" may sound great in a song, but I got tired of that wind—always blowing, everywhere.

The pervasiveness of the wind is also a characteristic of the Holy Spirit. David asked, "Whither shall I go from thy spirit?" and proceeded to describe the all-pervasiveness of the Holy Spirit (Psalm 139:7-12). Men have opposed His moving in every age. Sometimes religious leaders, and sometimes even well-meaning but ignorant Christians, have attempted to hold Him back. But you can't put a rope around the wind. Jesus said, "The wind blows wherever it pleases" (John 3:8, *NIV*). The Holy Spirit is going to move!

THE SPIRIT MOVED IN GOVERNMENTS

In the Old Testament, the Holy Spirit moved upon men to direct them in government. He moved in their minds to give them wisdom and ability. It is recorded in Numbers 11 that 70 men were chosen to partake of the Spirit that was upon Moses. When this happened, they prophesied. However, two of these men remained in camp and did not attend the ceremony. The Spirit, nevertheless, fell upon them also, and they prophesied (vv. 16, 17, 24-26). The Holy Spirit is sovereign and, like the wind, He blows where He pleases!

The Spirit came also upon kings. A notable example of this is King Saul. He prophesied vigorously and long. It became a proverb among the people: "Is Saul also among the prophets?" (1 Samuel 10:12). Another example is King David. When he summed up his life, the greatest honor he ever received was expressed in the words "The Spirit of the Lord spake by me" (2 Samuel 23:2). The sovereign Spirit moves upon whom He will, with apparent disregard to the opinions of men in the matter.

THE SPIRIT MOVED ON THE PROPHETS

Beyond government—with higher authority—the prophets spoke as they were moved by the Holy Ghost. Nehemiah 9:30 records the words of the Levites in prayer concerning Israel: "You . . . testified against them by Your Spirit in Your prophets" (*NKJV*). In the New Testament, Peter said, "For the prophecy came not in old time by the will of man: but holy men of God spake as they were moved by the Holy Ghost" (2 Peter 1:21).

Being "moved by the Holy Ghost" is the force reflected in the words of the prophet Isaiah: "The Lord spake thus to me with a strong hand" (8:11). This vigorous, dynamic, active, and activating Person is revealed throughout the Old Testament. The last book, Malachi, closes with the promise of yet another prophet to come. Filled with the Spirit from his mother's womb, John the Baptist burst forth on Israel, marking the closing days of the Old Testament dispensation (Matthew 11:13, 14).

THE SPIRIT MOVED IN PEACEFUL WAYS

Often the "Restless One" rested. In an odd turn of the Hebrew language, the word *rachaph* sometimes meant "to be still." This seems the opposite of "to move," but the apparently opposing ideas are reconciled in the image of a brooding hen that flutters and then settles down on her eggs.

This image is portrayed in the cloud that led Israel in the wilderness (Numbers 9:15-23). The cloud would stop and hover over the place where the Israelites were to camp. Numbers 10:36 says, "And when it rested, [Moses] said, Return, O Lord, unto the many thousands of Israel." Ancient rabbis, puzzled about the cloud, finally concluded this "Shekinah" was none other than the Spirit of God, moving and resting as God led His people.

This cloud foreshadows the New Testament "communion of the Holy Ghost" (2 Corinthians 13:14). The church, "builded together for an habitation of God through the Spirit" (Ephesians 2:22), experiences those special times when the nearness of the Spirit rests upon the congregation and simply shuts out the world. There is a closeness to God as the Spirit settles over the congregation. At these times, the "wind" of God is not sweeping in forceful demonstration but is like the refreshing that causes the weary to rest (Isaiah 28:12).

The Passover lamb, typifying Jesus, was required to be shut up by the family four days before sacrifice. The Holy Spirit insists on that special fellowship of the Spirit. A beautiful chorus we used to sing describes it well:

> Shut in with God in the secret place,
> There in the Spirit beholding His face.
> Gaining new power to run in the race.
> I love to be shut in with God.

"He that dwelleth in the secret place of the most High shall abide under the shadow of the Almighty" (Psalm 91:1). We must have these times of quiet when we hear His "still small voice." We come from these times with the sweet incense of the Spirit clinging to us, just as the garments of the priest before the golden altar of the Tabernacle had the aroma of incense.

CONCLUSION

When Noah released a dove after the flood, it returned with a green leaf in its beak (Genesis 8:8-11). This beautiful symbol of the Holy Spirit proclaimed the waters of judgment were past and a new beginning had come. The Holy Spirit is always interested in new beginnings. He was there like a wind in the beginning of Creation (Genesis 1:2). Here He is symbolized by a dove.

The dove is a peaceful bird. However, it is fiercely jealous of its territorial rights and will fight to maintain them. The Holy Spirit stakes out a claim on our lives when we are born again, and He is at cross-purposes with the flesh and the world system: "For the flesh lusteth against the Spirit, and the Spirit against the flesh" (Galatians 5:17). The Holy Spirit is "the Spirit of holiness," and calls us to forsake the world system and enjoy the fellowship of God as sons and daughters of God.

With the Spirit resting on us and heaven's fragrance clinging to us, it is time again to move with the moving Spirit and go forth to the battle for truth. When the cloud lifts and moves on, like Moses we cry, "Rise up, Lord, and let thine enemies be scattered" (Numbers 10:35).

QUESTIONS

For Thought:

1. In what ways may we refer to the Holy Spirit as "the Restless One?"

2. The Holy Spirit is called "the Wind of God." How is He like the wind?

3. How many instances can you remember when the Holy Spirit moved like wind in the Bible?

4. What role did the Holy Spirit play in the giving of God's Word?

For Discussion:

1. Have a qualified person explain to the group Biblical Creation and the role of the Holy Spirit in God's original creative acts.

2. Discuss some examples of the Holy Spirit's moving on government officials in the Old Testament.

ACTIVITIES

1. This week, relate to someone an instance of a particular "move" of God in the life of an Old Testament prophet.

2. Share with others an experience in which you knew the Holy Spirit moved in a "peaceful way."

Chapter 3

Symbols of the Holy Spirit

1. List three popular trademarks or logos used today by businesses. How do these symoblize products?

2. List some symbols of the Holy Spirit used in the Bible. Why did God use symbols to teach us about the Holy Spirit?

SYMBOLS OF THE HOLY SPIRIT

by
Homer G. Rhea

Scripture: Luke 3:22

INTRODUCTION

A symbol is a visible sign or representation of an idea, a quality, or another object. Religious symbolism, then, suggests a deeper spiritual meaning than a literal interpretation might depict. The Holy Spirit is characterized in the Bible by various symbols—*fire, wind, water, a dove, a seal,* and *oil.* Each of these symbols we will consider have a message for us.

FIRE

John the Baptist was mightily used of God, and many thought him to be the Messiah. But John denied that this was so and drew a sharp contrast between himself and Christ. In fact, he said that he was not worthy even to carry the shoes of the Master, a task the lowliest slave would be expected to do.

John also contrasted the baptisms offered by Jesus and himself. His baptism was with water unto repentance, but Jesus would baptize with the Holy Spirit and fire (Matthew 3:11). The water baptism was important and spiritual in character, but only the Son of God, who had completed the work of redemption and returned to the Father, could pour out the Holy Spirit.

In the Upper Room on the Day of Pentecost, the believers saw tongues of what looked like fire separating and settling on the head of each person (Acts 2:1-4). In *The Miracle of the Holy Spirit*, Charles Allen observed: "John saw it on Peter; Andrew saw it on Nathaniel; James saw it on Mary; and on around the entire group. No one was left out. Each was given a witness of his own. It came not only upon the Lord's twelve chosen apostles, not only upon the seventy who had been commissioned as evangelists, but upon every believer."

Fire symbolizes the divine presence. It also represents fervor and enthusiasm. It speaks of that divine energy that is available to every believer and with which we can be effective workers in God's kingdom. Thus Jesus associated our power with God with the Holy Spirit's coming into our lives (see Acts 1:8).

Those who were present in the Upper Room were filled with the Holy Spirit. To be filled with the Spirit is to be brought completely under His control. Paul illustrated this when he admonished, "Be not drunk with wine, wherein is excess; but be filled with the Spirit" (Ephesians 5:18).

Also, they spoke in other tongues as the Spirit enabled them. How beautiful is God's working when man gives his full cooperation. The happenings of the Day of Pentecost are irrefutable evidence of that.

WIND

The prophet Ezekiel was instructed to prophesy to the wind (ch. 37). Thus far his prophesying had been only to the dry bones in a valley. God had honored his obedience, and the bones had come together to form bodies. But they still had no life in them.

Therefore, Ezekiel was told to prophesy to the wind so that the breath of God might "breathe upon these slain, that they may live" (v. 9). He felt encouraged to obey God because of what had happened earlier when he had prophesied to the dry bones. Because they had come together as God had said, he could then conclude that when he prophesied to the wind, it would breathe life into the bodies—as God had said.

From Ezekiel's experience, we learn that what God has done in the past is an indication of what He will do again. In fact, whatever God has done in the past, we can trust Him to do again under the same circumstances.

When Ezekiel obeyed the command of the Lord, breath came into the dead bodies and they began to live. Alive, they stood up on their feet, and they formed an exceedingly great army. They then faced new life, a new beginning, new dimensions, new horizons.

Not until afterward did the Lord begin to explain to Ezekiel the meaning of this experience (v. 11). Thus far Ezekiel had simply obeyed God without fully understanding the significance of either God's commands to him or his obedience to them. Now the Lord began to unfold His purpose and to explain the symbolism of what the prophet was witnessing. He told him that the bones represented "the whole house of Israel." The Hebrews were in exile—far from the land they loved. Their homes had been destroyed; their Temple lay in ruins. But they had demonstrated a remarkable ability to survive and adjust. As a matter of fact, that had become the crux of the problem. They were managing so well—even prospering—in their new life in Babylon that their initial despair had turned first into resignation and finally into self-satisfied, comfortable complacency. But although they were doing quite well physically and materially, they were spiritually dead.

The Lord declared that He would bring His people up out of their graves—in essence, He would resurrect them from their exile and bring them back to the land of Israel. This promise was partially fulfilled in the return of a remnant of Israel to their homeland from Babylonian captivity. But there was a broader meaning to the raising of the dry bones. It spoke also of the dispersion of the Jews that took place in A.D. 70 and of their second restoration to the homeland, which was given official recognition when Israel again became a state in 1948.

Physical restoration to the homeland is only a portion of what God has in store for His people. He also has spiritual blessings for them. The day will come when they will "know that I am the Lord" (v. 13) and that the Lord has brought them into the land. They will receive no glory for themselves. The spirit of pride and arrogance will be replaced by the spirit of humility and submission. Then will come Israel's most glorious era. Even the kingdom of Solomon in all its splendor cannot be compared to this period.

One could not have told by looking that the exiles in Babylon were spiritually dead. From all appearances they were thriving. No doubt, they would have readily acknowledged that they believed in God. Although we may *look* healthy, we each need to turn our vision inward and ask ourselves, "Am I spiritually dead?" Without the Spirit—the *wind,* the *breath*—of God in our lives we have no hope of contributing anything of eternal value to the world or of accomplishing any everlasting good. We need the wind that blew at Pentecost to imbue us with life and make us an army of Spirit-filled witnesses for Christ.

Since the Jews who had relocated to other areas returned annually to Jerusalem for the Day of Pentecost, there was always an international presence there for that festival. While the masses were gathered in Jerusalem to observe the Jewish festival, about 120 believers were gathered in the Upper Room awaiting the coming of the Holy Spirit, whom Christ had promised to send.

Suddenly, as they were waiting, these believers heard a sound from heaven like the blowing of a violent wind. Living in this area, they had witnessed many storms at sea, and they had heard the blowing of violent wind many times. What they heard was the same sound, but this sound came out of a clear sky. They were sure of one thing—it came from heaven.

In the Scripture, the Holy Spirit is often symbolized by wind. In Ezekiel's vision of the valley of dry bones, the wind symbolized the life-giving, energizing power of the Spirit. In His conversation with Nicodemus, Jesus used the wind as a symbol of the life-giving work of the Spirit. On the Day of Pentecost, the wind again symbolized the Spirit; it indicated His power—mighty, mysterious, heavenly, but unseen.

WATER

In John 7:37-39, the apostle described an event that took place on the final and most important day of the Feast of Tabernacles. Jesus' customary posture for teaching was to sit down, but on this occasion He stood up. It appears that He assumed a solemn attitude and spoke in a more elevated tone of voice than ordinary: "If any man thirst, let him come unto me, and drink. He that believeth on me, as the scripture hath said, out of his belly shall flow rivers of living water."

Jesus extended an invitation to thirsty souls to come to Him to have their thirst quenched. Thirst represents spiritual needs. In the Sermon on the Mount, Jesus said: "Blessed are they which do hunger and thirst after righteousness: for they shall be filled" (Matthew 5:6). For every thirsty heart, Jesus will be a fountain of living water.

The believer who drinks of this living water becomes himself a fountain. He will be so filled that He overflows to others. What a beautiful scenario: The waters first spring forth from Christ himself and then from those whose thirst Christ has quenched and whom He has filled with His presence and grace.

John said that Jesus had the Holy Spirit in mind when He spoke of quenching spiritual thirst and having rivers of living water flowing from within. Only after the Day of Pentecost did the disciples witness the manifestation of spiritual gifts which served to point men to new life in Christ. The author of Hebrews wrote, "How shall we escape, if we neglect so great salvation; which at the first began to be spoken by the Lord, and was confirmed unto us by them that heard him; God also bearing them witness, both with signs and wonders, and with divers miracles, and gifts of the Holy Ghost, according to his own will?" (Hebrews 2:3, 4).

Then John gave a before-Pentecost and after-Pentecost picture. He said that the Spirit had not yet come because Jesus had not yet been glorified. He also said that those who believe were to receive the Spirit. This does not mean that the Spirit was not already active. Prior to the Day of Pentecost, the Spirit had acted on men both in the Old Testament and in the circle of disciples; but He was not yet *in them* as a possession, working in their personal lives. Neither could He be, for Jesus said, "Nevertheless I tell you the truth; It is expedient for you that I go away: for if I go not away, the Comforter will not come unto you; but if I depart, I will send him unto you" (John 16:7). With the Spirit's coming is the promise that He will quench spiritual thirst. Thus, water symbolizes the effectiveness and sufficiency of the Spirit's ministry.

DOVE

Can you imagine what John must have felt when Jesus came to him to be baptized? The Baptist was at the height of his ministry when Jesus left Galilee, where He had lived so many years, and came to the Jordan to be baptized by him. Christ's coming indicated that He understood the hour of His messianic mission had come and it was time for Him to act.

When Jesus expressed His desire to be baptized by John, John protested strenuously. In his commentary on Matthew, R.C.H. Lenski wrote: "John's treatment of Jesus is the very opposite of that accorded the Pharisees and the Sadducees. These he refused to baptize on account of their sins and their impenitence. Jesus he refused to baptize because of His sinlessness and because of his own sinfulness." He acknowledged a need to be baptized by Jesus and was astonished that Jesus, instead, came to him to be baptized.

In the first recorded words of Jesus since He spoke to His mother when He was 12 years old, He answered John's objection and declared this was the right thing to do; it was necessary to fulfill all that God required. Lenski observed: "He, the Sinless One, the very Son of God, chooses to put Himself alongside of all the sinful ones for whom John's sacrament was ordained. He thus connects Himself with all instances of John's baptism; for it is His mediation that makes these truly efficacious for sinners. By thus joining Himself to all these instances of John's baptism, He signifies that He is now ready to take upon Himself the load of all these sinners, [in other words] to assume His redemptive office."

By His baptism in water, Jesus identified Himself with, and committed Himself to, the work of redemption. After the baptism was finished, the subsequent events—the heavens opening, the dove descending, and the voice of the Father speaking—signified the divine acceptance of Him for this work.

The heavens, which had been closed, opened to Jesus. He is indeed the door by which we find entrance into the regions beyond this temporal, mortal life. Because of Him, the barrier between God and man has been removed.

The Spirit of God descended in the form of a dove and rested upon Jesus. The dove figure symbolizes the friendliness, purity, innocence, meekness, and graciousness of the Spirit. His descent marked the Lord's anointing for ministry. Later, Peter would say, "God anointed Jesus of Nazareth with the Holy Ghost and with power: who went about doing good, and healing all that were oppressed of the devil; for God was with him" (Acts 10:38).

The Father identified Jesus as His Son, whom He dearly loved and in whom He found delight. This announcement of love for the Son came as Jesus was about to do the Father's will in the great work of redemption.

SEAL

In Ephesians 1:13, Paul offered a spiritual history of the people to whom this letter was written. Although they were Gentiles, they were included in the scope of the gospel. They heard the gospel preached and believed its message. Then they were sealed with the Holy Spirit, whom God had promised.

A seal is a mark of ownership. It was stamped on wax to authenticate a document. A seal—in the ordinary sense of an outward mark, badge, or impression—would be placed on the outside of things; but the Holy Spirit also puts His stamp within us—upon the heart. His indwelling enlightens, guides, and transforms the believer. He is the most appropriate sign of God's presence and ownership of us.

This divine seal comes from God to those who are in Christ. Believers have a special stamp upon them. Only they can fully appreciate the security this gives them, for the blessings the Holy Spirit brings to them are only a foretaste of what is to come.

The apostle reaffirmed the importance of the role of the Spirit in redemption. He has sealed us for the day of redemption. He is the personal pledge of our eventual full redemption—the time when we arrive at a state of complete conformity to the will and image of Christ.

To what extent are you living under the control of the Spirit? There are two kinds of teachers: those who teach orally and those who teach by example. The most powerful teaching is done by example. This kind of teaching does not require extraordinary speaking ability. It only requires a good, clean, wholesome life. This kind of life is within the reach of every follower of Christ. As we are yielded to Him, He takes charge of our life and enables us to live victoriously. The Holy Spirit, who has stamped His seal within us, provides the strength and stamina for us to set a Christian example that others may be attracted to the Lord. What kind of teaching are you doing?

OIL

Under divine guidance, Samuel took a flask of oil and poured it on Saul's head, anointing him to be leader over Israel (1 Samuel 10). This practice of anointing was common in Israel and indicated the separation of a person or thing for special service. Thus, the stone at Bethel (Genesis 28:18), the ark (Exodus 30:26), priests (Exodus 28:41), prophets (1 Kings 19:16), as well as kings, were consecrated in this fashion.

After the anointing, Samuel gave Saul a threefold sign of confirmation.

The prophet told him that he would meet two men near Rachel's tomb who would tell him that the donkeys he sought had been found; that he would meet three men going up to Bethel who would greet him and offer him two loaves of bread; and that he would go to Gibeah, where he would meet a procession of prophets who would be prophesying. Then, he told Saul, "The Spirit of the Lord will come upon thee, and thou shalt prophesy with them, and shalt be turned into another man" (1 Samuel 10:6).

Although God anointed Saul for his role as king of Israel, Saul failed to walk in obedience to God and therefore fell into divine disfavor. The Lord sent Samuel to the house of Jesse to anoint one of his sons to succeed Saul as king (1 Samuel 16). At first, Samuel thought Eliab was God's choice. Although Jesse's oldest son had made a favorable impression on Samuel, the Lord said Eliab was not to be the king. God's concern was not with the physical appearance of the man (the height of his stature—if He were, Saul would have been ideal) but rather with the inner qualities of character, leadership, and obedience.

When David was brought before Samuel, the Lord told the prophet that this lad was to be king. When Samuel anointed him, the Spirit of the Lord came upon David in power. The Spirit provided him with the divine equipment he needed to perform his role as king of Israel.

In Zechariah 4, the prophet described a vision he had seen—a solid gold lampstand with a bowl at the top. It had seven lights on it and two olive trees by it, one on the right of the bowl and the other on the left. The angel who was talking with Zechariah said that what he saw signified the need for the power of the Holy Spirit in the fulfillment of God's work. The word of the Lord to Zerubbabel was that success comes "not by might, nor by power, but by my spirit, saith the Lord of hosts" (v. 6).

The clear lesson of this passage is that human resources are not adequate to do the work of the Lord. Physical strength, wealth, and military force alone will not achieve the divine mission. There must be the anointing of the Holy Spirit—which is symbolized by oil.

This is not to say that human resources have no place in God's work. As a rule, God does not build without them. But it is a combination of human resources and the help of the Holy Spirit that results in amazing accomplishments. Paul wrote, "For we are labourers together with God" (1 Corinthians 3:9).

Not only is the work of the Lord accomplished through the combined efforts of the divine and the human, but it is also wrought through the unified efforts of laymen and clergy. Zechariah wanted to know the meaning of the two olive trees and the pipes out of which poured golden oil. The reply was, "These are the two anointed ones, that stand by the Lord of the whole earth" (Zechariah 4:14). The two anointed ones are generally recognized as being Joshua, the high priest (3:8; 6:11), and Zerubbabel, the civil head of the nation. Both needed the Holy Spirit's help; and when that help was granted, each would be involved in causing God's light to shine amid the darkness of this world. The world today still needs that light emanating from all believers.

The Holy Spirit lives in believers, possessing them fully in order to shine out and to flow out from them. This is the normal experience of Christians when they are right with God.

CONCLUSION

F.E. Marsh, in his book *Emblems of the Holy Spirit*, makes a comment about each of the symbols included in this study. He sees *fire* as a symbol of "the purification and penetration of the Spirit's operations," *wind* proclaims "the winnowing and searching of the Spirit's power," *water* symbolizes "the effectiveness and sufficiency of the Spirit's ministry," the *dove* speaks of "the beauty and gentleness of the Spirit's character," the *seal* indicates "the security of the Spirit's grace and the proprietorship of His love," and *oil* is typical of "the Spirit's grace and the illumination of His teaching."

The various functions of the person and work of the Holy Spirit are made clearer by considering these Biblical symbols.

QUESTIONS

For Thought:

1.   Review the five characteristics of the Spirit as symbolized in the dove.
2.   The Holy Spirit "seals" believers. What does this mean to you?
3.   Ask God to fill you with His Spirit today.

For Discussion:

1.   In what ways are water baptism and Spirit baptism similar? Different?
2.   Why do you suppose God chose fire as a prominent symbol of the Holy Spirit?
3.   Explain in your own words the meaning of Ezekiel's use of the wind as a symbol of the Holy Spirit.
4.   Discuss the twofold use of water as a symbol of the Spirit in John 7:37-39.

ACTIVITIES

1.   This week, watch for symbols that will remind you of the Holy Spirit.
2.   God also speaks to us in a "still small voice." In your devotions this week, listen for His voice speaking softly to you.
3.   Recall an incident from your own experience when the anointing of the Holy Spirit made the difference in your circumstances. Thank God for this and similar occasions.

Chapter 4

THE HOLY SPIRIT AND CHRISTIAN LIVING

One often has to work in an impure environment.   How can one "stay on top" and keep himself pure in thoughts, motives, and actions?

THE HOLY SPIRIT AND CHRISTIAN LIVING

by
Mark L. Williams

Scripture: John 16:8-11

INTRODUCTION

Without a doubt the 20th century will be remembered in Christendom as a century of the Holy Spirit. Perhaps at no other time in human history has the church of the Lord Jesus Christ witnessed such a visible, global inbreaking of the Holy Spirit's power. The outpouring of the Spirit on a group of people worshiping at a schoolhouse in Cherokee, North Carolina, in 1896; the outpouring under Charles Parham in Topeka, Kansas; the outpouring in Moscow, Russia, and Seoul, Korea; the outpouring upon those gathered at the Azusa Street Mission in Los Angeles, California; the outpouring in Oslo, Norway, and Stockholm, Sweden; the healing revivals during the decade of the '50s; the outpouring of the Spirit during the Charismatic Renewal, which swept millions of people into the kingdom of God—these and so many other testimonies signify that the Holy Spirit is at work in our day. In the words of the psalmist, "This is the Lord's doing; it is marvellous in our eyes" (Psalm 118:23, KJV).

But while we celebrate the visible manifestations of power, we tend to overlook the practical impact of the Holy Spirit on daily living. The mighty demonstrations of power are not an end in themselves but a means to an end, that is, that men and women might be saved and live the Christ-life.

THE IDENTITY OF THE HOLY SPIRIT

To understand the work of the Holy Spirit we must first understand who He is. The Holy Spirit is not a force, an instrument, an attitude, an atmosphere, an influence, or a phantom. The Holy Spirit is a person. He is divine. He is the third person of the triune Godhead, coequal, coeternal, coexistent with God the Father and the Lord Jesus Christ.

His divinity is set forth by the position in which He is placed with relation to the Holy Trinity. In his benediction to the church at Corinth, the apostle Paul placed the Holy Spirit together with God the Father and the Lord Jesus Christ, saying, "May the grace of the Lord Jesus Christ, and the love of God, and the fellowship of the Holy Spirit be with you all" (2 Corinthians 13:14).* Additionally, Jesus Christ commissioned the church to make disciples, "baptizing them in the name of the Father and of the Son and of the Holy Spirit" (Matthew 28:19). When confronting Ananias and Sapphira about their sin against the Holy Spirit, Peter said, "You have not lied to men but to God" (Acts 5:4). In each of these scriptures the Holy Spirit occupies a position of equality with the other members of the Trinity.

His divinity is also established by the attributes which He possesses. He is omniscient, omnipresent, and omnipotent. The prophet Isaiah proclaimed the Holy Spirit to be "the Spirit of wisdom and of understanding, the Spirit of counsel and of power, the Spirit of knowledge and of the fear of the Lord" (11:2). There are no limits to His knowledge, for it is He who knows "the deep things of God," and reveals them to us (1 Corinthians 2:9-12). He is *omniscient*—all-knowing—which enables Him to teach the believer "all things" and to guide into "all truth" (John 14:26; 16:13).

Not only is the Holy Spirit all-knowing, but He is also *omnipresent*—everywhere-present. The psalmist asked, "Where can I go from your Spirit? Where can I flee from your presence?" (Psalm 139:7). He is "the eternal Spirit" Jesus promised would abide with us forever (Hebrews 9:14; John 14:16).

Besides being omniscient and omnipresent, He is also *omnipotent*, which means He is all-powerful! Throughout the Bible we see His power displayed as the agent of Creation, inspiration, Incarnation, and victory. It is this power that caused the angel to say, "For nothing is impossible with God" (Luke 1:37).

Equally important to the identity of the Holy Spirit is His personhood. He bears and exhibits all the marks of personality. He possesses the characteristics of mind (Romans 8:27), will (1 Corinthians 12:11), understanding (1 Corinthians 2:10, 11), and emotion (Ephesians 4:30). He engages in activities such as speaking (Revelation 2:7), interceding (Romans 8:26), teaching (John 14:26), commanding (Acts 16: 6, 7), appointing (Acts 20:28), testifying (John 15:26), and leading (16:13). He can be grieved (Ephesians 4:30). He can be lied to (Acts 5:3). He can be insulted (Hebrews 10:29). He can be blasphemed (Matthew 12:31, 32). All of the characteristics of personhood belong to Him.

For this reason we should be careful to never address Him with the neuter pronoun *it*. The Holy Spirit is not an "it." He is a person. He is the Spirit of the living God!

THE INVOLVEMENT OF THE HOLY SPIRIT IN REGEN-ERATION

Though the Holy Spirit is a divine person in the Trinity, He never draws attention to Himself. His intention is to point men and women to Jesus Christ. He testifies of Christ (John 15:26), imparts the teaching of Christ (14:26), and brings glory to Christ (16:14). In short, the Holy Spirit has been sent into the world to bring men and women into relationship with Jesus Christ and to empower them for Christian service.

This was the whole point of Jesus' teaching in John 16:7-11. In this context Jesus was preparing His disciples for His departure and the coming of another Comforter, the Holy Spirit. To describe this Comforter's mission, Jesus said, "When he comes, he will convict the world of guilt in regard to sin and righteousness and judgment: in regard to sin, because men do not believe in me; in regard to righteousness, because I am going to the Father, where you can see me no longer; and in regard to judgment, because the prince of this world now stands condemned" (vv. 8-11).

The Holy Spirit initiates the whole process of redemption by bringing about conviction. Since the days of Noah, the Holy Spirit has been in the business of convicting, striving, and pleading with men and women to turn to God in repentance and faith. In the words of Matthew Henry, the Holy Spirit convinces the world "of the fact of sin, of the fault of sin, of the folly of sin, of the filth of sin, and lastly, of the fruit of sin." Jesus said, "He will convict the world of guilt in regard to sin" (v. 8). In this regard He makes us aware of our responsibility and need of a Savior.

The Holy Spirit deals not with just the symptoms but with the basic nature of sin, which is unbelief. Verse 9 says, ". . . in regard to sin, because men do not believe in me." Only the Holy Spirit can reveal the essential nature of sin. Sin, in its essence, is unbelief in our Lord Jesus Christ. Sin therefore is rebellion against God—rebellion against His will, His Word, and His way—the only way of salvation.

Not only does the Holy Spirit convict of sin, but He also convinces of righteousness. If there is any word which describes the essential character of Jesus Christ, it is *righteous*. He is Jesus Christ the Righteous. His death was vindicated by His ascension to the right hand of the Father. In light of His righteousness, our self-righteousness appears as filthy rags. Through repentance and faith we are made the righteousness of God in Him (2 Corinthians 5:21). Our righteousness is guaranteed by His position at the Father's right hand and His intercessory prayers.

The Holy Spirit also convicts the world "in regard to judgment, because the prince of this world now stands condemned" (John 16:11). Jesus said, "Now is the time for judgment on this world; now the prince of this world will be driven out" (John 12:31). The Cross did that! The devil's works were destroyed. The fear of death was conquered. The prince of this world is driven out! His captives are freed by Jesus Christ!

Not only does the Holy Spirit convict of sin, but He also serves as the agent for regeneration. That is, He actually facilitates and transacts the new birth! This was the message of Paul in Titus 3:5: "He saved us, not because of righteous things we had done, but because of his mercy. He saved us through the washing of rebirth and renewal by the Holy Spirit."

The new birth, being born again, is a birth by the Spirit in which a sinner is re-created and made anew with a new nature. In His conversation with the religious leader Nicodemus, Jesus said that to enter the kingdom of heaven you must be "born of water and the Spirit" (John 3:5). In verse 8, Jesus used the phrase "born of the Spirit." Regeneration is an experience wrought by the Holy Spirit in which He ushers us into the kingdom of God.

It is the Holy Spirit who shows us the need of a Savior (John 16:8-11). The Holy Spirit also draws us to Jesus Christ and enables us to confess that Jesus is Lord, for "no one can say, 'Jesus is Lord,' except by the Holy Spirit" (1 Corinthians 12:3). It is the Holy Spirit who applies the atoning work of Jesus Christ to our hearts and baptizes us into

---

Salvation prepares us for heaven; the baptism in the Holy Ghost prepares us for Kingdom service on this earth.

Christ: "For we were all baptized by one Spirit into one body—whether Jews or Greeks, slave or free—and we were all given the one Spirit to drink" (12:13). He identifies us as children of God: "We know that we live in him and he in us, because he has given us of his Spirit" (1 John 4:13).

Every Christian has the Holy Spirit abiding with him or her in a measure. After all, the apostle Paul said, "If anyone does not have the Spirit of Christ, he does not belong to Christ. . . . Those who are led by the Spirit of God are sons of God. For you did not receive a spirit that makes you a slave again to fear, but you received the Spirit of sonship. And by him we cry, 'Abba, Father.' The Spirit himself testifies with our spirit that we are God's children" (Romans 8:9, 14-16).

What is the difference between being saved and being baptized in the Holy Spirit? While the Holy Spirit is at work in both of these experiences, there is a distinct difference between the two in terms of agency and purpose. At salvation, we are born of the Spirit (John 3:8), but in Spirit baptism we are baptized in the Spirit (Matthew 3:11; Acts 1:5). In salvation, the Holy Spirit is the agent (Titus 3:5; 1 Corinthians 12:13); in the baptism in the Holy Ghost, Jesus Christ is the agent (John 1:33). Salvation prepares us for heaven; the baptism in the Holy Ghost prepares us for Kingdom service on this earth. At salvation we receive power to become the children of God (John 1:12); the baptism in the Holy Ghost gives us power to be witnesses to the uttermost parts of the earth

(Acts 1:8). Salvation is a gift for sinners (Ephesians 2:8); the Holy Spirit baptism is a gift for believers (John 7:38; Acts 2:38).

Having convicted us of sin and facilitated the transaction of the new birth, the Holy Spirit then seals us. Paul wrote in Ephesians 1:13, 14: "And you also were included in Christ when you heard the word of truth, the gospel of your salvation. Having believed, you were marked in him with a seal, the promised Holy Spirit, who is a deposit guaranteeing our inheritance until the redemption of those who are God's possession—to the praise of his glory."

What does it mean to be sealed by the Holy Spirit? In Biblical times a seal indicated ownership, it signified a finished transaction, and it validated authority. Likewise, the seal of the Holy Spirit upon us indicates the genuineness of the regenerative act of God in our hearts; He signifies that the transaction has been completed and we now belong to God! Our bodies have now become temples of the Holy Spirit!

THE INDWELLING OF THE HOLY SPIRIT

This leads to one of the most startling revelations in Scripture concerning the ministry of the Holy Spirit. In 1 Corinthians 3:16 Paul asked, "Don't you know that you yourselves are God's temple and that God's Spirit lives in you?" Again, in 1 Corinthians 6:19, he asked, "Do you not know that your body is a temple of the Holy Spirit, who is in you, whom you have received from God"? We have become dwelling places of God—habitations of God through the Spirit. The Holy Spirit has set up residence within us and our bodies are now His temples!

What a marvelous thought! The same Spirit that covered and filled the Tabernacle (Exodus 40:34), the same Spirit which came and filled the Holy of Holies with Shekinah glory when Solomon's temple was fully dedicated to God (1 Kings 8:10, 11), is the same Spirit and glory that indwells us as believers! We are no longer arenas for entertainment, libraries for research, or offices for commerce. We are temples. The Holy Spirit lives within, and all that we do is hallowed by His presence.

It is important to understand that when the Holy Spirit moves in, He does so not to set up residence as a guest but as a manager. When He comes, He takes charge. He renovates, restores, and renews. He immediately sets out to evict sin and death and undo their terrible damage. Not only do our spirits undergo this renovation but also our very bodies. "And if the Spirit of him who raised Jesus from the dead is living in you, he who raised Christ from the dead will also give life to your mortal bodies through his Spirit, who lives in you" (Romans 8:11). Our bodies, which are inching their way toward certain death, are being readied for resurrection. The same God who raised Jesus has sent His Spirit to make our resurrection possible.

As a temple of the Holy Spirit we have a sobering responsibility. That responsibility is to keep our temple clean. This is the meaning of 1 Corinthians 6:18: "Flee from sexual immorality. All other sins a man commits are outside his body, but he who sins sexually sins against his own body." That responsibility includes Colossians 3:5: "Put to death, therefore, whatever belongs to your earthly nature: sexual immorality, impurity, lust, evil desires and greed, which is idolatry." Furthermore, Paul said, "But now you must rid yourselves of all such things as these: anger, rage, malice, slander, and filthy language from your lips. Do not lie to each other, since you have taken off your old self with its practices and have put on the new self, which is being renewed in knowledge in the image of its Creator" (vv. 8-10). Other responsibilities of the Spirit-filled life are included in 2 Corinthians 6:14—7:1:

> Do not be yoked together with unbelievers. For what do righteousness and wickedness have in common? Or what fellowship can light have with darkness? What harmony is there between Christ and Belial? What does a believer have in common with an unbeliever? What agreement is there between the temple of God and idols? For we are the temple of the living God. As God has said: "I will live with them and walk among them, and I will be their God, and they will be my people. Therefore come out from them and be separate, says the Lord. Touch no unclean thing, and I will receive you. I will be a Father to you, and you will be my sons and daughters, says the Lord Almighty."

Since we have these promises, dear friends, let us purify ourselves from everything that contaminates body and spirit, perfecting holiness out of reverence for God.

CONCLUSION

Our challenge and responsibility is to stay clean in a dirty place! One day a very young minister was being escorted through a coal mine. At the entrance of one of the dim passageways, he spied a beautiful white flower growing out of the black earth. "How can it blossom in such purity and radiance in this dirty mine?" the preacher asked. "Throw some coal dust on it and see for yourself," his guide replied. When he did, he was surprised— the fine, sooty particles slid right off the snowy petals, leaving the plant just as lovely and unstained as before. Its surface was so smooth that the grit and grime could not adhere to it. In commenting on this incident, an unknown author says, "Just as that flower could not control its environment, so we cannot help it that we have to live in a world filled with evil. But God's grace can keep us so clean and unspotted that though we touch sin on every side, it will not cling to us."

*All scriptures are from the *New International Version*, unless otherwise indicated.

QUESTIONS

For Thought:

1. What are some of the characteristics of personhood that the Holy Spirit possesses?
2. While it is God's forgiveness and grace that cleanses us, what is our responsibility for purifying ourselves (see 2 Corinthians 7:1)?
3. Meditate on how one can stay clean in a dirty place.
4. Since the Holy Spirit is "everywhere present," should this cause you apprehension or comfort? Why?

For Discussion:

1. Discuss the role of the Holy Spirit in regeneration.
2. Discuss the difference in "being saved" and "being baptized in the Holy Spirit."
3. What are some things we are responsible for, in light of the fact that we are temples of the Holy Spirit?

ACTIVITIES

1. This week, tell the story of the "white flower in the coal mine" to someone you know.

2. Follow up with your personal testimony of God's "keeping-grace" in a particular difficulty.

Chapter 5

BAPTISM IN THE HOLY SPIRIT

1. What does the phrase "tarry for the Holy Spirit" mean?
2. Is it necessary to tarry in order to be baptized in the Holy Spirit? Explain.

BAPTISM IN THE HOLY SPIRIT

by
Sam McGraner

Scripture: Acts 2:1-4

INTRODUCTION

The cool crisp air of the Judean morning was suddenly broken by the sensation that now had become familiar to Joel. It was the anointing of Jehovah, the God of heaven and earth. Once again He was calling Joel to his clay tablets to carefully inscribe a message, a prophecy to be given to His people. But this time it was not a message of the desolation of the locusts; it was not even a command to "blow the trumpet" and call a "solemn assembly." This time the voice of Jehovah was speaking of a more far-reaching event, an occasion to take place at some point in the future that would be far different from any other moment in time. "And it shall come to pass afterward" Jehovah said, "that I will pour out My Spirit on all flesh; your sons and your daughters shall prophesy, your old men shall dream dreams, your young men shall see visions. And also on My menservants and on My maidservants I will pour out My Spirit in those days" (Joel 2:28, 29).*

❖ ❖ ❖ ❖ ❖

The sun had now fully risen over the city of Jerusalem on this day

— 55 —

of the great feast. For seven days we had been gathered together as we had been instructed to do. We had been in prayer and in discussions of important matters; but we had also been in unity of spirit and mind. Andrew, ever the observant one, was the first to notice it—the sound of wind in the rafters. But quickly all took notice of it, for it became the sound of a rushing mighty wind. The house was filled with the sound of that wind, and we all sat in awe.

Just as the sound of the wind had come, so did the flames—first appearing as a great single blaze of many flames, then separating into many individual flames that descended and came to rest upon each of our heads. My thoughts rushed so quickly. I remembered the words of Christ just prior to His ascension: "But tarry in the city of Jerusalem, until you are endued with power from on high" (Luke 24:49). Yes, this must be what He intended for us to receive.

Just at that moment, feeling as I had never felt before, I began to speak aloud with tremendous joy and elation. But I did not understand what I was saying. The others who were gathered with us began to speak in strange languages as well. What a wonderful and stirring event this had become. Many came running together to see what was taking place; and among these, a number of Cyrenean pilgrims to the Feast of Pentecost gathered around me and listened intently as though they understood these strange words I was saying.

Then Peter stepped forward, speaking with more eloquence and power than I had ever heard him speak before:

> Men of Judea and all who dwell in Jerusalem, let this be known to you, and heed my words. For these are not drunk, as you suppose, since it is only the third hour of the day. But this is what was spoken by the prophet Joel: "And it shall come to pass in the last days, says God, that I will pour out of My Spirit on all flesh; your sons and your daughters shall prophesy, your young men shall see visions, your old men shall dream dreams. And on My menservants and on My maidservants I will pour out My Spirit in those days; and they shall prophesy" (Acts 2:14-18).

It had been a typical Sunday evening service at our church in the small Kentucky mountain town of Vicco. I had finished my prayer during the altar service and had returned to my seat when the Holy Spirit began to move on a sister who was seeking for the baptism in the Holy Ghost. As I looked on, Gladys Browning, a stalwart lady of the church, instructed me to go pray with the sister seeking for the Baptism. This seemed unusual to me, for I had not as yet received the Holy Spirit baptism myself. But Gladys was not one you could easily say no to, so I did as she had asked. In a few moments, the Holy Spirit was moving upon me as I had never experienced before. As I interceded for the one seeking for the Baptism, I myself was caught up in the moving of the Spirit. Suddenly my lips and my tongue were no longer under my control. They began to utter words that were unintelligible to me, phrases that were not my own but all the same were as natural and comfortable to me as though they were words of my own choosing. What a glorious experience! What a life-changing event! Just as I had been changed on the day of my new birth, I had once again received a transforming experience. I was bolder, fuller, somehow more able not only to be a Christian but also to proclaim the goodness of Christ.

It was May 1982 and I was in Grand Junction, Colorado, for a conference on the Holy Spirit, one of many conducted around the nation during that period. I had delivered a message on the baptism in the Holy Spirit and had given an invitation for those who desired this gift from God to come to the altar. Two Native American women came forward along with several others. I soon learned that the older of the two was the mother of the younger and spoke only Navajo, her native language. Her daughter, who was already a Spirit-filled believer, served as our interpreter as we prayed. It was very interesting to listen to her pray in Navajo as she tarried for the gift of the Holy Spirit. And then the moment came—there was a distinct change in her language as well as in her countenance. Joy gleamed from her face as she raised her arms and continued to speak in this language that was as strange to her as hers had been to me. Her daughter joyfully exclaimed, "She has received the Holy Spirit."

In these four vignettes, we glimpse the spectrum of the wonderful phenomenon that we call the baptism in the Holy Spirit. The first two are historical happenings of which we can only imagine the details. The second two are from my own personal experiences. The fulfillment of Joel's prophecy of long ago is a verifiable reality in our world today. His will and His plan are that the church be a Spirit-led and Spirit-filled body, that the baptism in the Holy Spirit should not be the exception among us but the rule.

This experience is for all believers.

THE PROMISE

When Joel wrote the prophecy of the outpouring of the Holy Spirit, he was familiar with the Holy Spirit's power. The working of the Holy Spirit in the lives of men had been well chronicled in Old Testament literature by the time of Joel. The Old Testament is filled with stories of Spirit-empowered men and women who set for Joel and for us examples of what God can do through those yielded to Him.

As I read the Old Testament accounts of the Holy Spirit's coming upon men like Samson, David, and many others, I am impressed with the power and scope of this promise. Scripture does not ascribe to Samson unusual size or muscularity that are typically ascribed to him today. His enemies were puzzled about the source of his strength. By an unseen power, however, Samson performed all his mighty feats of strength—a strength not of man nor of this world but a miraculous strength wrought by the Holy Spirit upon him. David was an ordinary shepherd, one of such youth that not even his own father, Jesse, thought to call him from tending the sheep when Samuel came to anoint one of his sons to be king. Yet, it was he who was anointed after Samuel asked that he be summoned from the flocks. After this anointing, we are told that "the Spirit of the Lord came upon David from that day forward" (1 Samuel 16:13). By virtue of the presence of this Spirit, he would become the mighty warrior and king that we now know him to have been.

The promise of God given through Joel was that this same Spirit would one day be poured out upon "all flesh." Not just a Samson or a David, as the occasion arose, but any and all of God's servants would have access to this promise. Notice Joel's designations of candidates–all flesh . . . sons . . . daughter . . . old men . . . young men . . . menservants . . . maidservants. Can there be anyone omitted in this promise? Are there any among us who cannot see themselves somewhere in Joel's vision?

As the time for the fulfillment of the promise drew near, it pleased God to reaffirm the prophecy of Joel, first by John the Baptist and then by the Lord himself. John was confronted with the expectation of the masses for the coming of the Messiah. They wondered if John himself might be the One. His rejection of this idea was accompanied with a renewal of the prophecy of Joel, for he said, "I indeed baptize you with water; but One mightier than I is coming. . . . He will baptize you with the Holy Spirit and fire" (Luke 3:16). Jesus later confirmed the words of John, emphasizing the imminence of this event. He told His disciples to "wait for the Promise of the Father, 'which,' He said, 'you have heard from Me; for John truly baptized with water, but you shall be baptized with the Holy Spirit not many days from now'" (Acts 1:4, 5). The culmination of a vital part of God's plan of grace was about to come to pass.

THE FULFILLMENT

Without a doubt, the most important events in all of history are the birth, death, and resurrection of Jesus Christ. Very close to these in importance, however, stands the occasion of the initiation of the Spirit-filled, Spirit-empowered, Spirit-led church. Jesus' presence was one of power, stability, authority, and courage as He led His disciples from His baptism by John to His ascension on the Mount of Olives. It was His presence that had facilitated the miracles, that had fed the multitudes, and that had delivered the Word in such a way that it would be said of Him, "No man ever spoke like this Man!" (John 7:46). Yet during His life with these chosen disciples, He would prepare them for His departure and for the coming of "another Helper"—the Comforter.

Jesus told His disciples of His impending departure from this world and gave to His disciples (then and now) some of the most stirring words of the Gospels (John 14—17). Interspersed in this discourse are several references to "another Helper," or "another Comforter" (KJV), whom the Father would send when the Son had returned to the Father. Jesus heralded the importance of this Helper with these words: "It is to your advantage that I go away; for if I do not go away, the Helper will not come to you; but if I depart, I will send Him to you" (16:7). As important and meaningful as His own presence was to His disciples, Jesus knew the presence of the Holy Spirit would be even more advantageous to His followers. The fulfillment of this promise is therefore paramount in importance.

Surrounding the fulfillment of the promise are several elements that we might call precedents—Biblical facts that we can assume are important to the fulfillment of the promise. The first of these comes from the words of Jesus himself: "Behold, I send the Promise of My Father upon you; but tarry in the city of Jerusalem until you are endued with power from on high" (Luke 24:49). The key word here is *tarry*. In our day of fast food and convenience stores, we have fallen prey to taking the same type of approach to our faith. Church and faith today for many must be as quick and easy as our food and shopping. But tarrying bears a much different message. The Lord was resurrected the third day after Passover and seen of the disciples for another 40 days (Acts 1:3), which leaves seven days from His ascension until Pentecost. These were the days of tarrying. The general description of how they spent these days are summed up in Acts 1:14: "These all continued with one accord in prayer and supplication." The outpouring that took place on the Day of Pentecost followed seven days of tarrying specifically identified as "prayer and supplication." These were not idle days of waiting, but days of earnest entreaty for the promised Helper, or Comforter, to come. A precedent is set, then, for us to *tarry*.

There is a social precedent—*unity*—set for us as well. These disciples had come together in obviously united obedience to the instructions of Christ to tarry in Jerusalem. But that unity was not simply an act of obedience; it became the posture of the gathering. In Acts 1:14 and 2:1, at the beginning of the tarrying period and at the end, they are said to have been "with one accord." Their unity becomes for us a precedent that would require us to put away our differences so that the Holy Spirit might have a unified body to work through. What an important and powerful precedent this is. The manifestation of fire that appeared to them seems to have been a reflection of the need for this type of unity. The "divided" ("cloven," KJV) tongues of fire seem to have appeared first as a single blaze which divided and rested upon each in the room. The Spirit is not divided, and He needs a unified church to work through so that the blaze of God's power might have its full impact.

Another precedent set at Pentecost is that of *personal transformation*. Among the evidences of this transformation, we might consider the somewhat abstract concepts of spiritual boldness, or spiritual anointing; but the first and most obvious evidence is that of tongues. Acts 2:4 very clearly states, "And they were all filled with the Holy Spirit and began to speak with other tongues, as the Spirit gave them utterance." As Joel had prophesied, this outpouring was not selective but included all those who had gathered in the Upper Room. Each of them received evidence in a very personal way that something dynamically different had taken place within their own being. It was a spiritual experience, of course, but it had a physical manifestation as well. The tongues of those present became instruments of the Holy Spirit. This was no quiet and sedate manifestation. It must have been quite noisy indeed, for it attracted a "multitude" of those in Jerusalem.

And finally, a wonderful precedent of *evangelism* was established that day, for we are told that through the witness of the Holy Spirit "about three thousand souls were added to them" (v. 41). The ultimate objective of the Holy Spirit experience is not to thrill the recipient or to elate the crowd, but to bear witness to the gospel of Jesus Christ. This should become the goal of everyone who receives this experience—to see others brought into the kingdom of God and be filled with the Spirit.

God's anointing of Peter by the Holy Spirit on this occasion brought a message of fulfillment: "This is what was spoken by the prophet Joel" (v. 16). This is it! You need look no further nor wait any longer. You may now place this promise of God on the list marked FULFILLED.

THE EXPERIENCE

The prophetic promise and its historic fulfillment fail to elicit my full appreciation until I realize that this same experience is intended for me also. Although the baptism in the Holy Spirit is for every believer and though it is intended to be a universal blessing among members of the body of Christ, it is at the same time an intensely personal experience.

It is no small thing for the strong human spirit to yield its control and will to that of the Holy Spirit. Yet that is exactly what must take place in order to receive the Holy Spirit baptism. For me to submit my heart, my thoughts, the very secret things of my life to the Holy Spirit that He may inhabit my being and control my actions is to become more personal with the Holy Spirit than I have ever been with any person on earth. This may very well explain the reason many do not receive the baptism in the Holy Spirit. The fear of losing personal autonomy is very real. But any reluctance can be overcome through the observance of Biblical precedents.

To one degree or another, every Spirit-filled person has at some point complied with the Biblical precedents found at the fulfillment of Joel's prophesy in the Book of Acts. We each tarried before God in prayer and supplication, brought ourselves into harmony with other believers, manifested the evidence of tongues at our baptism in the Spirit, and were made greater witnesses of God's grace in the process.

The idea of tarrying before God may have become out-of-date for some, but the Biblical precedent still stands. Nothing creates a hunger for the presence of God, generates a right attitude, and subdues the stubborn human spirit more than an extended time of prayer and supplication before God than *tarrying*. As a gift, the baptism in the Holy Spirit cannot be earned; but as an experience, it cannot be procured without cost. The 120 tarried for seven days before the Holy Spirit experience came to them. Paul, after he was blinded by the heavenly light, spent three days in Damascus praying and fasting, before Ananias came to him, that he might receive his sight and be filled with the Holy Spirit (Acts 9:1-18). It was in direct response to the prayers and fasting of Cornelius that Peter was sent to him, that he and his household might receive the Holy Spirit (Acts 10). The precedent is there. If the experience of the baptism in the Holy Spirit is what you desire, then tarry for it. The Holy Spirit will come to those who tarry for Him.

It is important also to remember that the Biblical precedent is one of unity—they were "with one accord" when the Spirit came. Disunity is the greatest hindrance to the moving of the Holy Spirit in the church. It restricts the Spirit's filling of new converts and limits His refreshing of those already filled. How disappointed God must be when we cannot set aside petty differences in order to allow the Spirit to do His work. A truly Spirit-filled church with a desire for Holy Spirit revival will endeavor to maintain a Biblical unity conducive to the Spirit's presence. In the absence of discord or argument, we have the positive influences of joy and peace that compose an important part of this experience of the Holy Spirit baptism. In a spiritually unified, joyful, and peaceful church environment, the experience of the baptism in the Holy Spirit will be the rule and not the exception.

After being threatened for preaching, Peter and John rejoined the rest of the disciples and prayed for boldness to continue preaching the gospel (Acts 4). After their prayer, "They were all filled with the Holy Spirit" (v. 31). What took place can best be described as a refreshing, or renewing, of the same experience they had received on the Day of Pentecost.

It might be concluded, then, that we have the same opportunity and obligation—that we too should be occasionally refreshed and renewed by the power of the Spirit. The baptism in the Holy Spirit is a continuing, lifelong experience subject to frequent renewal in personal devotions and worship. This is the spiritual walk so often mentioned by Paul. To him it seemed vital that every Christian be constantly "filled with the Spirit" (Ephesians 5:18).

THE SCOPE

As Jesus was about to leave His disciples to return to the Father, He gave them a few words of insight into the future and scope of the church: "But you shall receive power when the Holy Spirit has come upon you; and you shall be witnesses to Me in Jerusalem, and in all Judea and Samaria, and to the end of the earth" (Acts 1:8). With the baptism in the Holy Spirit comes the power to be witnesses of Jesus, and that witness will reach to "the ends of the earth" (*NIV*). But was Jesus speaking only to those who were there with Him at His ascension? Or did He intend the message for a larger audience?

The answer to these questions can be found in the first Pentecostal message ever preached. Peter, under the anointing of the fresh outpouring of the Holy Ghost, told the onlookers in Jerusalem: "Repent and be baptized, every one of you, in the name of Jesus Christ for the forgiveness of your sins. And you will receive the gift of the Holy Spirit. The promise is for you and your children and for all who are far off—for all whom the Lord our God will call" (Acts 2:38, 39, *NIV*). Peter's message was that the gift of the Holy Spirit was not limited to those who heard Jesus make the promise but was also extended to those who now had heard and believed their witness of Jesus on the Day of Pentecost.

It can be easily argued from Scripture that wherever the witness of Jesus Christ is believed, the promise of the baptism in the Holy Spirit is extended. From major urban areas to the smallest villages, from the most refined populations to the most primitive—everywhere the gospel of Jesus Christ is preached, the promise of the Holy Spirit baptism is valid. As did Joel, Peter identified candidates for this experience. He stated that the promise is for "you . . . your children . . . all who are far off . . . all whom the Lord our God will call" (*NIV*). Again, all can find themselves somewhere among the candidates listed.

The message of salvation in Jesus Christ is intended for all. That wonderful word *whoever* in John 3:16 omits no one from God's offer of grace. If all are included in the scope of grace, all are also included in the scope of the gift of the Holy Spirit. The baptism in the Holy Spirit is being received throughout the entire world today in spite of national, cultural, and language barriers. "All whom the Lord our God will call"—"all flesh"—are being endowed with this marvelous experience in our day. Just as Jesus said, the Holy Spirit is empowering believers to witness to "the ends of the earth."

CONCLUSION

The baptism in the Holy Spirit should not be looked on as something for only an elite group within the church. It is a gift of God intended for all believers, to empower them for the service of the kingdom of God.

*All scriptures are from the *New King James Version* unless otherwise indicated.

QUESTIONS

For Thought:

1. What can you do to unify your church and enhance the free flow of the Spirit?

2. Spirit-baptized people in Acts 2 were immediately transformed. Meditate on the transformation in your life which resulted from the same experience.

3. What Biblical precedents can we follow to promote the expansion of the church?

For Discussion:

1. Discuss the universality of Joel's prophecy.

2. What are some meanings implied in the word *tarry*?

3. The Holy Spirit's influence on the church is extensive and primary. Discuss how the Spirit empowers believers.

ACTIVITIES

1. If you have not received the baptism in the Holy Spirit, seek for it this week.

2. If you have received the Holy Spirit, pray for someone you know who has not yet received this promise.

3. Share your experience (or that of someone you know) in receiving the baptism in the Holy Spirit

Chapter 6

POWER FOR SERVICE

Serving Christ by Serving Others

1. Compare Peter's life before and after his baptism in the Holy Spirit.
2. Can we expect the same dramatic changes in our lives? Explain.

Serving Christ
by Serving Others

POWER FOR SERVICE

by
Gerald J. Johnson

Scripture: Luke 24:49

INTRODUCTION

Power for service resides in the baptism in the Holy Spirit. Spirit-baptized believers obey God by sharing in His work. Consequently, His divine power is released in service. Divine energy becomes effective when it is used for the purpose for which it is directed. Faith and obedience release this divine power in active energy toward human need. The Word of God gives hundreds of assurances of the Holy Spirit's empowering presence to ensure effective service.

Christian service is too sacred to be motivated by money and too difficult to be motivated by duty; only love will suffice. The New Testament, a Holy Spirit-inspired Pentecostal document, preserves a record of Christian service in the early church. Church history records the post-apostolic ministry of the Holy Spirit—up and until the return of Christ for the church. We need this supernatural power for service today.

JESUS PROMISED SUPERNATURAL POWER
(Luke 24:49; Acts 1:8)

"Behold, I send the Promise of My Father upon you: but tarry in the city of Jerusalem until you are endued with power from on high" (Luke 24:49).*

"You shall receive power when the Holy Spirit has come upon you" (Acts 1:8).

Jesus taught the supernatural scope and sequence of the Holy Spirit's ministry. The doctrine of the Holy Spirit occupies a prominent place in Scripture and stands in the forefront of redemptive truth. Christ taught the inviting, the indwelling, and the infilling of the Holy Spirit. He promised the Holy Spirit would be with, in, and upon believers. "He dwells with you and will be in you" (John 14:17).

The Holy Spirit invites—He is with us. Jesus promised the Holy Spirit would be with His disciples in conviction and conversion. "And when he is come, he will reprove the world of sin, and of righteousness, and of judgment: Of sin, because they believe not on me" (John 16:8, 9, KJV). The Holy Spirit imparts living faith which is the gift of God (Ephesians 2:8). This results in the miracle of being born from above (John 3:3-7). It results in the believer's being baptized into the body of Christ (1 Corinthians 12:13).

The Holy Spirit produces a new creation—with a new orientation, a new direction, and a new destination (2 Corinthians 5:17).

The Holy Spirit indwells—He is in us. Jesus promised the Holy Spirit would be in believers in sonship and sanctification. This aspect of the Holy Spirit's ministry is stated when Christ said, "He will be in you" (John 14:17). The experience was made possible after Christ's resurrection. "He breathed on them, and said to them, 'Receive the Holy Spirit'" (John 20:22).

The Holy Spirit was given to them as a witness to their sonship after Christ was resurrected. "As many as received him, to them gave he power to become the sons of God" (John 1:12, KJV). "And because you are sons, God has sent forth the Spirit of His Son into your hearts" (Galatians 4:6).

Paul wrote, "But you are not in the flesh but in the Spirit, if indeed the Spirit of God dwells in you" (Romans 8:9). The indwelling of the

Spirit, reproducing the Christlife in the believer, brings forth the growth of Christian character and conduct called the "fruit of the Spirit" (Galatians 5:22, 23).

The Holy Spirit infills—He comes upon us. Jesus promised the Holy Spirit would come upon the believers for witnessing and soulwinning purposes. Before the Day of Pentecost, the Holy Spirit is pictured as coming upon men and women for a specific work for which they were chosen. God gave His promise through Joel (2:28-32) that in the last days God would pour out His Spirit upon all flesh. Jesus said His anointed ambassadors would be witnesses, after the Spirit came upon them.

The purpose of the Holy Spirit's coming upon them was to make them effective witnesses of the great salvation, "which at the first began to be spoken by the Lord, and was confirmed to us by those who heard Him, God also bearing witness both with signs and wonders, with various miracles, and gifts of the Holy Spirit" (Hebrews 2:3, 4).

The Holy Spirit baptism is clearly the "upon-ness" power for service given to God's anointed ambassadors.

JESUS SENT THE HOLY SPIRIT (Acts 2:1-4)

The Holy Spirit came upon all of them. The promise given by Christ was fulfilled suddenly. They were all with one accord and they were all filled. The result of their being suddenly overwhelmed by the Spirit's power was that they "began to speak with other tongues as the Spirit gave them utterance" (Acts 2:4). This is a supernatural sequence of experience, expression, and expansion—both individually and corporately. They heard them speak in 18 different languages "the wonderful works of God" (v. 11). They were so overwhelmed with power from on high that their physical behavior resembled intoxication (v. 13).

The prophecy of Joel 2:28, "on all flesh," was fulfilled, and they were all filled full! The original recipients were numerous and varied. Mary, the mother of Jesus, along with His brethren and the women who followed Him, received the same power for service. They were all filled full of the power necessary to fulfill their cameo roles in the great drama of redemption.

Believers were empowered for service irrespective of temperament, culture, or difference in personality. The Book of Acts records that they all received the identical spiritual experience. Among those originally empowered were Peter, the impulsive; James, the ambitious; John, the intense; Matthew, the precise; Nathaniel, the guileless; Simon, the revolutionary; Thomas, the skeptical; Andrew, the practical; Mary and others of like faith.

Later, multitudes of believers received the Holy Spirit empowerment for service. There were despised Samaritans, educated Pharisees, Roman officers, students in schools of Alexandria, and citizens of Greek cities. All these believers received the promise of power. The promise was immediately and conspicuously fulfilled. The change that the power of the Spirit made in the courage of these believers is very noticeable. Jesus had suddenly multiplied Himself by several thousand believers. He stamped His own deathless personality upon each of them. Thousands of voices were testifying to His resurrection and singing His praises in Jerusalem. They were empowered ambassadors after the Spirit came upon them. Their irrepressible boldness is evidenced by their words: "We cannot but speak the things which we have seen and heard" (Acts 4:20).

God started a spiritual revolution on the Day of Pentecost. These empowered believers were living proof "that the kingdom of God is not meat and drink; but righteousness, and peace, and joy in the Holy Ghost" (Romans 14:17, KJV). They were an assembly of the anybodies, a company of the committed, eternity's expendables, the faithful few, the Master's minority. These were living exhibits that eternal results come "'not by might nor by power, but by My Spirit,' says the Lord of hosts" (Zechariah 4:6).

Their powerful, anointed service was manifested in their words, hands, shadows, clothing, and embraces. The Holy Spirit, the Almighty Advocate, made it all possible. The divine inbreaking of the Spirit was not "this or that," or "this and that," but "this is that!" It meant power for evangelism. This is that power for service promised and sent by the Lord.

The Scriptural description is sevenfold: the empowered believers were ambassadors representing (2 Corinthians 5:20), branches bearing fruit (John 15:5), epistles instructing (2 Corinthians 3:2), lights illuminating (Matthew 5:14), salt preserving (Matthew 5:13), stewards distributing (1 Peter 4:10), and witnesses testifying (Acts 1:8). As they experienced Kingdom power, they expressed it and extended the Kingdom.

BELIEVERS MINISTERED IN THE POWER OF THE SPIRIT (Acts 2:14-18)

The Holy Spirit empowerment for service brought a realization of God's presence, a reproduction of His holiness, and a reenactment of His power. The disciples were suddenly filled with boldness, utterance, power, and optimism. The clarity and force of their message caused the multitudes to cry out, "What must we do to be saved?" (see Acts 2:37). "And with great power the apostles gave witness to the resurrection of the Lord Jesus" (4:33).

Peter and John were warned not to preach in the name of Jesus. Peter answered, "We cannot but speak" (4:20). This seems incredible, in view of his recent denial before a servant girl. We are confronted at once in Acts with the presence and activity of the Holy Spirit in the lives of the newly baptized. They were empowered to go beyond themselves, becoming primarily concerned with the happiness, welfare, and well-being of others. We observe them loving automatically and spontaneously, without regard to the so-called worldly worth or excellence of the person who happened to be standing in front of them at a given moment. They received power to think Christ's thoughts, to live Christ's life, and to work Christ's works.

Peter is an important apostolic personality in the Book of Acts. God had expectations for Peter above his doubts and fears. God's Spirit moved him beyond his adolescent spiritual level. Peter is a model of a human who failed, yet subsequently succeeded in his Christian calling. What God claimed, Peter yielded. What he yielded, God accepted. What God accepted, He filled; and what God filled, He used mightily for His glory.

The Scriptures record the dramatic changes in the life and service of the apostle Peter after the Holy Spirit's empowerment for service. God's power enabled Peter to confront Jewish tradition, Roman power, and Greek culture. He triumphed over every foe after the Holy Spirit came upon him.

Before Pentecost, Peter was tentative: "Lord, if it is You, command me . . ." (Matthew 14:28). After his Spirit baptism, he was certain: "This is that. . . !" (see Acts 2:16).

Before, he was self-resourceful (Mark 14:29); afterward, he was God-dependent (Acts 3:16).

Before, he was self-acting (Luke 22:50); afterward, he was Christ-activated (Acts 4:10).

Before, he was cowardly (Luke 22:56-60); afterward, he was bold in spirit (Acts 4:13).

Before, he was a swearing man (Matthew 26:74); afterward, he was a praising man (Acts 2:47; see also 4:21; 5:41).

Before, he warmed by the world's fire (John 18:18); afterward, he was motivated by an inner fire (see Acts 2:14).

Before, he was self-authorized (John 21:3); afterward, he was Spirit-energized (Acts 4:8).

Peter's "before" and "after" transformed him from selfishness to service.

A new era began at Pentecost. This change became the closing word of Peter's messages in Acts 3 and 4. Peter preached that God's Spirit was active in them to multiply the wondrous works of God. The baptism in the Holy Ghost initiated them into the moving of God, involving them directly with God's purposes in their generation. The baptism in the Holy Ghost became the blessed anointing that abides and is permanent (see 1 John 2:20). We know that we remain in Him and He in us because of His Spirit which He has given to us (1 John 4:13)

The Holy Spirit urged the apostles and believers to carry out their witness in the world. Their testimony had great value. God used their testimony to help change the context and makeup of eternity. The Spirit's empowerment within them impelled them to anointed service.

Paul, apostle to the Gentiles, is a prominent Pentecostal personality. He founded the church at Ephesus, usually regarded as the finest church in the New Testament. Paul's power for service is noted in his farewell address in Acts 20:16-38.

Paul desired to celebrate the Feast of Pentecost in Jerusalem. He cited numerous examples of the Holy Spirit's empowered service among the Ephesians. Paul noted his manner of life (v. 18), his compassionate service (v. 19), his uncompromising teaching (v. 20), his bold evangelism (v. 21), the Holy Spirit's leadership (vv. 22, 23), his unflinching courage (v. 24), their unbroken fellowship (v. 25), his audacious claim (vv. 26, 27), his unceasing warning (vv. 28-31), his releasing of the saints (v. 32), his pure motive (vv. 33, 34), his sacrificial giving (v. 35), his family prayer (v. 36), and his farewell embrace (vv. 37, 38).

Paul knew that there was no power without service. He modeled faith-action service. Paul served in expectation of God's faithfulness. The power within did not mean that he was more effective than his brethren. However, Paul was more effective than he would have otherwise been. His role became complete as he walked in the reality of Holy Ghost anointing. Paul would have been less than God intended without the Pentecostal power for service. Power became evident when he performed God-given service. He became conscious of God's strength as he used it. Paul knew the reality of God in Ephesus as he engaged the Enemy in the field of service. The manifold grace of God at Ephesus in Acts 20 was Spirit-directed.

POST-APOSTOLIC MINISTRY AND BEYOND (Acts 2:39)

"For the promise is to you and to your children, and to all who are afar off, as many as the Lord our God will call" (Acts 2:39).

Laypeople were also entrusted by God with the task of communicating the gospel and making new disciples. Holy Spirit-empowered laypeople carried out the Great Commission for the first three centuries of the Christian movement. The Holy Spirit used the people of God to attract multitudes of citizens of the heathen empires away from their idols and into the Christian faith.

The state took on the responsibility of making its people Christian, beginning with the fourth century and the rule of Constantine. Many generations during the Middle Ages experienced very little soulwinning service. Later, the Reformation teaching on the individual priesthood of believers sparked some soulwinning service. The Catholic Counter-Reformation of missionary monks began sharing the Roman Catholic versions of Christianity. For many decades, Protestantism had virtually no one doing soulwinning service.

Protestantism rediscovered the Great Commission in the 18th century. Believers understood that the Holy Spirit empowerment for service was not intended for the original apostles only. God raised up gifted servants. Pastors ministered in local communities. Evangelists reached out to nations and cultures. Missionaries took the good news to unreached nations and cultures. In late 19th century, the church experienced another Pentecostal outpouring. Today, over 100 years later, millions of laypeople around the world are Holy Spirit-baptized, and they now know that service and soulwinning are the central roles of the Christian life. We now know that if the world is to be won to Christ and

His kingdom, it will be won by laypeople and gifted leaders empowered by the Holy Spirit.

The ultimate triumph of the gospel is sure. The winds of New Age ideologies cannot snuff out the Light of the World. But God has not made us accountable for the ultimate victory of Christ. God has given us the task of serving and winning our generation. We can succeed in the task if we are empowered by the Holy Spirit.

The Holy Spirit makes serving and soulwinning a passion before it is a program. This passion of the heart results in saving action. Power for service is the experience one receives when Christ fills with the Spirit. Power for service is the expression of a Christ-centered heart. Power for service is the extension of a Christ-mastered will. The impact is personal, local, continental, hemispheric, and worldwide.

SUPERNATURAL SPIRITUAL POWER FOR SERVICE TODAY (2 Timothy 3:16, 17)

The assertions of God's Word concerning Holy Spirit baptism and power for service in our day are authentic. The unimpeachable sources in God's Word are authoritative. The verifiable evidences of God's Word are applicable. These truths of God's Word about Holy Spirit baptism are experienced objectively because the Word says so; they are experienced subjectively by His witness within; and they are experienced empirically because He works in powerful service through the Spirit-baptized believer (see 2 Timothy 3:16, 17).

The working of the Holy Spirit is a contemporary movement, not a monument. The Spirit baptism is not a goal to be reached but a gate of service to be entered. The Holy Spirit baptism is the Spirit's creative ability to release divine energy through the believer and give away life. Spirit baptism expresses itself in prophetic, powerful, practical, and personal service.

Prophetic service (Acts 2:14-21). The Holy Spirit's immanent presence and Christ's imminent return are inseparably linked as we approach the end of the church age. God is quickly finishing His work and cutting it short. The church possesses the only power to meet and overcome the combined forces of evil. God is providing a constant enduement of Holy Ghost power and divine wisdom that insures His body against decay, disorder, and death.

A recent Holy Spirit prophecy urged: "Run toward the Enemy; run into battle as My servant David did. For be assured—if you do not, I will bring the battle to you." We become conscious of God's strength as we engage in battle. We know the reality of God with us as we engage the Enemy on the field of battle. Saul and David were both anointed of God. Both men faced the Philistines in the Valley of Elah. But only one man stood up, believed God, and hurled the stone that brought a great victory. Saul could have done the same, for the same God anointed him. David's faith turned the power of God's name into energy that toppled the giant, Goliath. The power needed was available ever since his anointing. Faith realized the possibilities. God was with His anointed servant when faith came into action.

Our anointing is in the baptism in the Holy Spirit. We are God's living stones. God promises rapid expansion as the result of radical obedience.

The battle for world dominion has been joined. Peter stated that supernatural phenomena will be in evidence just before the Day of the Lord (Acts 2:19, 20). The Holy Ghost continues to burst upon the scene with a mighty end-time restoration. Jesus continues to do now what He had begun in the past (Acts 1:1). The church has an urgent mission marked by the expectation of the return of Christ. The church also has the indispensable enduement of power for Christian service (1:8). The Holy Spirit is a powerfully present person ready to give honor and glory to the glorified Christ and witness to His lordship.

We should look at the harvest with intensity coupled with a commitment to possess it. God is raising up lay practitioners and leaders who are obedient to His commands, strategy, and service. The Holy Spirit is moving the church closer to Jesus and out into the battle. Power is available to confront evil and the destructive supernatural forces that oppose Christ. God's people can count on His Word, wonders, and works to crash and smash the gates of hell (Matthew 16:18).

Powerful service (2 Corinthians 4:7). Men came dripping from the baptizing hands of John the Baptist. Believers still come blazing from the Holy Spirit baptism of Jesus. This powerful baptism of love includes love of enemies. Jesus enables this love miracle because when we love our enemies, there is no one left to hate. Jesus charges us to love them, and He takes the responsibility to change them. When we do what we should do, we always see God do what He alone can do. The truly fire-baptized believer cannot say, "Goodbye, Holy Spirit; see You at the next seminar or camp meeting." The Holy Spirit anointing abides. A cold, thirsty world needs a salty, fiery church empowered for service.

God is always active. Jesus said, "The Father works and I work" (see John 5:17), indicating ceaseless endeavor. The Lord is working through His body, the church. The Holy Spirit is moving now in powerful, ceaseless service. There is no possibility of our waiting for God; we can merely wait upon Him. God's power for service is inevitable when we are baptized in His Spirit. God never leaves the battlefield. We act upon His nearness. "We have this treasure in earthen vessels, that the excellence of the power may be of God and not of us" (2 Corinthians 4:7).

The Holy Spirit baptism in the believer turns water into wine. The believer pours out in another tongue initially, and boldly witnesses in the native tongue continually. The Holy Spirit baptism is causative: the outpouring precipitates an overflowing witness and testimony. "We are His witnesses . . . and so also is the Holy Spirit whom God has given to those who obey Him" (Acts 5:32). "The love of God is shed abroad in our hearts by the Holy Ghost" (Romans 5:5, KJV). This indwelling, outpouring, and overflowing love of God ministers to poor, broken, blind captives who thirst for Jesus, the Water of Life.

The Holy Spirit baptism is Biblical, not denominational. The Spirit's power for service is Scriptural rather than traditional. God is putting new wine in new bottles. There is no need of squeezing an old leather bag for a little wine when God is providing new wine, gallon after gallon, for the asking. He has saved the best wine for last in these last days' outpouring. It is better quantitatively than it was at the beginning. Greater works are being done because there are more people doing them in every nation on earth.

Those who experience God's power display strength, take spiritual action, and give spiritual instruction. Spiritual exploits abound today on every continent as we approach the return of Christ. The Holy Spirit moves us beyond our prevailing level of service and continually jolts our level of contentment. The Holy Spirit prompts the impulse to open our mouths boldly and give utterance to the good news that Jesus is alive, the devil is defeated, and God is in control.

Practical service (1 Corinthians 1:26-31). God will use anyone willing to be used. The greatest ability is availability. The Lord uses our relationships in life. What we receive we want to give away (John 1:35-42). God uses relationships to multiply, amplify, and glorify our lives.

The Lord uses our resourcefulness in life. We do what we can, find what is available, and turn it over to Jesus (John 6:1-14). Little is much when God is in it!

The Lord uses our reputation in life. We must be approachable, friendly, caring, and responsive (John 12:20-26). People must know that through us they can meet Jesus.

The Lord uses His reality in our lives. Testimony is the simple story of how God uses a believer—his faith, his commitment, and his communication. Our little will be much when God has all of it. We do the possible; God does the impossible. God uses our relationships, our resourcefulness, and our reputation as we let Him become the reality of our lives.

Personal ambassador service (2 Corinthians 5:20). Christian ambassadors act on behalf of God. God's Spirit-filled ambassadors are sent to represent the divine government on earth. We are official agents of the highest earthly rank during the day of Christ. We are authorized representatives and spiritual messengers of heaven's throne. We are divinely appointed to special service assignments. We are sent from the home office in heaven. We speak for the Creator and Sustainer of life. We reside in the "Life Embassy," the church. We carry out the divine orders in the Bible, God's "Book of Life." We pledge allegiance to the divine flag: His banner over us is love. We have the seal of God, the Holy Spirit of promise. We are accompanied by angelic hosts, the armies of Almighty God. We must warn the lost that we are in a "red-alert" status. It is the final alert before impending judgment.

The day of Christ will soon end. We must maximize our witness before the coming Day of the Lord. Nations recall their ambassadors before all-out war breaks loose. Soon, God will recall and remove His ambassadors from the earth just before the world enters into fiery judgment and experiences the final holocaust. The world must be told of repentance and righteousness. People must receive Christ to be robed and ready for Christ's return. We must tell the lost that God does not want to have heaven without them.

CONCLUSION (Peters 3:9)

Attention, all Spirit-baptized believers: Are you witnessing to the lost as God's anointed ambassador? If not you, *who*? If not here, *where*?

If not now, *when*? "Behold, He cometh!"

* Scriptures are from the *New King James Version* unless otherwise indicated.

QUESTIONS

For Thought:

1. Why do you think the Bible uses the symbol of baptism to describe the infilling of the Holy Spirit?

2. Why do you think the writer says that love should be the only motivation for Christian service?

3. What is the purpose and results of the Holy Spirit's coming "upon" believers?

For Discussion:

1. What pivotal changes did the Protestant Reformation bring in believers' view of the power of the Holy Spirit?

2. List and explain the seven descriptive terms for Spirit-empowered believers.

3. What are three things the Lord uses to multiply and amplify our practical service.

4. Discuss the meaning of the phrase, "personal ambassador service."

ACTIVITIES

1. Be a personal ambassador in your practical service this week Focus on one of the following:

    a. If your church has a jail or prison ministry, volunteer to participate this week.

    b. Visit a nursing home and share your testimony, talents, and time. Take a small gift to the person you visit.

    c. Share your food with someone who is in need this week.

Chapter 7

GIFTS OF THE HOLY SPIRIT

• Determine Them
• Develop Them
• Demonstrate Them

SPIRITUAL GIFTS

List the gifts of the Spirit which operate in your local church.

GIFTS OF THE HOLY SPIRIT

by
Paul O. Lombard Jr.

Scripture: 1 Corinthians 12:1-31

INTRODUCTION

Gifts! We start life on earth with gifts. Our mothers were given gifts in anticipation of birth. Each succeeding birthday means an occasion for gifts. Special occasions, achievements, Christmas, and marriage all call for the giving of gifts.

God also gives gifts. James 1:17 tells us, "Every good gift and every perfect gift . . . cometh down from the Father of lights, with whom is no variableness, neither shadow of turning." God's gifts are unique and costly.

The gift God gave to the world (John 3:16) is beyond estimate in terms of costliness. Jesus promised to pray that His Father would give us another priceless gift—the gift of the Holy Spirit (John 14:16).

In Luke 24:47-49, the church was promised special spiritual endowment to assist in carrying out the Great Commission. This prayer and promise was fulfilled in Acts 2 on the Day of Pentecost. The baptism in the Holy Ghost is a gift from God.

Baptism in the Holy Spirit in an individual's life opens the door for gifts to be bestowed on the church. We must understand that many experiences with God under New Testament covenants are conditional. For example, on the condition that we confess with our mouth the Lord Jesus Christ and believe in our heart that God has raised Him from the dead, we shall be saved (Romans 10:9). Conversely, those who do not believe will be lost. The same principle applies to the manifestation of spiritual gifts. The gifts of the Spirit cannot operate except as subsequent to the baptism in the Holy Spirit.

SPIRITUAL GIFTS TESTIFY (vv. 1-3)

Understand the difference between the "gift of the Holy Spirit" and the "gifts of the Holy Spirit." The *gift* is given in a baptismal outpouring, while the *gifts* are given to already Spirit-filled believers and exercised at various times.

The first statement Paul made in this chapter concerns knowledge of the Spirit. We must understand the meaning of "the Gift" before we delve into the blessings of "the gifts."

An overcoming church battles the power of darkness. It is a mistake to underestimate the tenacity and ferocity of demonic powers that assail the body of Christ. It is also a mistake to underestimate the power and authority that God has given the church to overcome the Enemy in battle. A powerless church is not in harmony with God's plan, for His Son purchased the church with His own blood.

Jesus gave us part of the divine plan in Matthew 16:18: "Upon this rock I will build my church; and the gates of hell shall not prevail against it." Paul provided part two in Ephesians 6:11 when he instructed us to "put on the whole armour of God, that ye may be able to stand against the wiles of the devil." So we see that God has a strategy of victory for the church. The composite picture is this: The church would be undergirded by solid rock. The body would be protected by impenetrable armor and endowed with dynamic gifts of the Spirit that testify of the power of God. This provides defense, offense, and foundational security.

What a contrast to the former religion of the Gentile church. Paul referred to the Corinthians' idols as "dumb," or silent. Idolatry is a recurrent theme in the Old Testament and cautioned against in the New Testament. Nowhere in the Bible does an idol ever communicate with a worshiper. Psalm 115 tells of idols who "have mouths, but they speak not" and "neither speak they through their throat" (vv. 5, 7).

But Israel's God speaks. Over and again He speaks. He speaks in the old covenant at "sundry times and in divers manners . . . unto the fathers by the prophets," and He speaks in the new covenant "by his Son" (Hebrews 1:1, 2). He speaks to the church by the written Word and oral gifts of the Spirit.

Paul also contrasted the emotionalism of heathenism in verse 2 with the Christian's confession of Jesus by the Spirit in verse 3. The validity of spiritual gifts is documented by the Holy Spirit's proclaiming Jesus as Lord.

The concept of Jesus Christ as Lord is resisted by our secular world. The unbelieving world equates Him on the same level as Muhammad or some kind of religious superstar. In essence, this is calling Him "accursed." The Holy Ghost, who is the Spirit of Truth, testifies of His lordship. If any spiritual gift cannot pass the doctrinal test of truth, it is not a witness of truth.

SPIRITUAL GIFTS EDIFY (vv. 4-11)

Diversity. We enjoy variety in food for our physical bodies. A delicious meal becomes unappetizing if served day after day without changing the menu. Church should never be dull and dead because the spiritual menu doesn't change. The bride in Song of Solomon 4:16 said, "Awake, O north wind; and come, thou south; blow upon my garden, that the spices thereof may flow out." Likewise, the church should yearn for the wind of the Spirit to blow upon the congregation the gifts that bring life to the body.

There are diversities of gifts from the fountainhead of the Spirit. Verses 4-6 talk about "diversities" but "the same." We see this principle in nature. Snow, ice, steam, and clouds are different in practical usage, but they are much the same since each is comprised of water. Temperature and atmospheric conditions determine what form the water takes.

Natural ability versus anointing. Paul was not referring to natural ability people are born with. He ascribed all of these diverse gifts to a common theme—they all come from one Spirit. Our greatest natural abilities are woefully inferior to the dynamic power of the Holy Spirit. Great oratory is no match for Spirit-anointed preaching or teaching.

When our Lord was on earth, He manifested a powerful ministry. When He entered into a town, He caused sickness, disease, devils, and death to become helpless. He spoke words, and the wind obeyed His command. He spoke words, and death was compelled to release people back to life. His hands distributed a lunch prepared for one boy and fed thousands of hungry people, plus each disciples returned to Him a basket of leftovers from his hands!

Gifts are not given to the church to enrich an individual or bring renown to someone's ministry. The purpose is edification for the body of Christ.

Authority and Miracles. Why would the Head of the church not expect the body to minister in power and authority? He knew this earthly sojourn was for a limited time. Jesus told His disciples in John 14:12: "He that believeth on me, the works that I do shall he do also; and greater works than these shall he do; because I go unto my Father." He fully expected His church to minister in power and authority. That's why God gave gifts to the church.

Experience teaches us wisdom and study increases our knowledge. Thus, an unbeliever can experience this as easily as a believer. But when wisdom and knowledge are administered by the Spirit as a gift, then the source is sovereign God.

Every person is given a measure of faith. Acts 16:31 shows us saving faith. Faith is also listed as a fruit of the Spirit. The gift of faith is a special faith that works miracles. The medical profession can cure sick bodies. In many cases the physical body has the ability to heal itself. The *gifts* (note the plural of this word) of healing are cures wrought in the supernatural. Again, we need to realize this is wrought by the Holy Ghost.

Jesus began His ministry with a miracle: "This beginning of miracles did Jesus in Cana of Galilee" (John 2:11). He closed His ministry on earth with a miracle (the ascension at Bethany). The Holy Spirit is present today to enrich the Body with gifts and miracles, affirming the gospel of Jesus Christ.

Prophetic voice. Men have stood on God's Word and uttered prophecies far beyond their comprehension. The church still has a prophetic voice for this world. Psychics, astrologers, and the occult are a bane to our generation. Why do they have audiences? Because people long to know the unknown. God absolutely forbade Israel to have any communication or fellowship with these works of darkness. God set the gift of prophecy in the church to reveal all we need to know by the Holy Spirit.

SPIRITUAL GIFTS UNIFY (vv. 12-31)

Unity and the human body. The human body is so dependent on each member that abnormality in the head can paralyze an arm or leg. An injury to the spine can immobilize the entire body. Nerves in the neck can affect nerves in the leg.

Paul used the human body to describe the unity of the Holy Spirit and our Lord's earthly church. He utilized this focus and analogy when he wrote to the church in Rome (Romans 12:4-8), to the church in Ephesus (Ephesians 4:4-13), as well as to the church at Corinth. He said in verse 27, "Now ye are the body of Christ, and members in particular." We are struck by the repeated use of the word *one* in this passage. In verses 12-14, Paul used the word *one* seven times. By verse 28, this one body is now manifesting eight ministries.

Unity and the Spirit. We see two measures of water in verse 13— baptism and a drink. We are baptized by the Spirit; at the same time we are filled as we drink! The word *all* in 1 Corinthians 12:13 corresponds to *whosoever* in John 3:16. Everyone and anyone—everywhere and anywhere—are invited to participate in God's plan of salvation and Spirit baptism.

The unity of this chapter is so complete that Paul shifted from the naming of the gifts in the first part to identifying them as individuals in the latter verses. We are reminded of the sovereignty of God as He selects those who will be set in the church as gifted (v. 28). God uses the same method of setting gifts in the church as He did in the Old Testament when He selected men for the priesthood in Israel. Hebrews 5:4 explains how it worked: "And no man taketh this honour unto himself, but he that is called of God, as was Aaron."

We are exhorted in 1 Corinthians 12:31 to "covet earnestly the best gifts," yet this chapter tells us more than once that it is the Spirit who makes the ultimate decision.

Unity, not uniformity. Unity does not demand sameness or uniformity. Unity can be enhanced by diversity. Take, as an example, a rainbow. Each color in the spectrum is beautiful on its own merits; but blended side by side in an arc in the sky, it is exquisite. Listen to the notes on a musical scale. Each note has a distinctive sound, but used together they produce musical harmony. One note struck has overtones. Notes struck in unison have unending overtones. It is said that the range of overtones on a symphony of notes has never been calculated.

Likewise, if one gift of the Spirit is dynamic in action, then the combination of many gifts in ministry overwhelms all the power of darkness. The unity of power adds up quickly when we consider the words of Moses that "one [can] chase a thousand, and two [can] put ten thousand to flight" (Deuteronomy 32:30).

CONCLUSION

The church is not to be a guardian of orthodoxy, but a people on a mission of deliverance to a lost world. For every kind of work the church must do, God has supplied a corresponding gift.

The church is a body with a Head, and the Head is far superior, in every aspect, to the rest of the body.

The church has sailed some stormy seas. Storms have the capability of splintering and fragmenting a ship. The infrastructure of gifts, helps, and government holds the fabric together during rough sailing.

The approximately 200 New Testament references to the subject of spiritual gifts are assurances of God's determination that the church will not fail for lack of power.

QUESTIONS

For Thought:

1. How does God speak to the church?
2. What is God's strategy of victory for the church?

For Discussion:

1. Explain the difference in "the gift of the Holy Spirit" and the "gifts of the Holy Spirit."
2. Contrast the difference in natural ability and the Holy Spirit's anointing through a spiritual gift.
3. Discuss the meaning of the phrase, "unity of the Spirit."
4. List some ways in which the church can exhibit and express unity while respecting diversity among believers.

ACTIVITIES

1. If God has gifted every believer in some way, how do you think He has gifted you?
2. Spend some time in prayer, meditating on the way or ways God has called or endowed you to do certain things in the body of Christ.

Chapter 8

MINISTRY GIFTS

1. What is "servant leadership"? Is the term contradictory?
2. What qualities can be recognized in a servant-leader?

MINISTRY GIFTS

by
Lane Lavender

Scripture: Romans 12:6-18

INTRODUCTION

The gifts of the Spirit are needed in the church today. All are equally important, but ministry gifts are especially essential. They produce the type of ministry needed to keep a church going and growing. For example, a local church could thrive without the gift of miracles in operation on a regular basis; however, it cannot survive without the gifts of teaching, giving, or governing.

The New Testament gives four lists of spiritual gifts: Romans 12:3-8; 1 Corinthians 12:8-10, 28-30; and Ephesians 4:11. Some say there are only nine gifts; others, 19. Many believers teach that the number of gifts is innumerable and not limited to the Scriptural lists. Some list the gifts by their nature (gifts of revelation, gifts of power, gifts of utterance); others, by their function (proclamation gifts, teaching gifts, service gifts, administrative gifts). Still others group the gifts by traveling gifts (apostles, teachers, evangelists); local gifts (pastors, governments, helps); public and private gifts; functional and official gifts; and the list could go on.

The seven gifts in Romans 12 are particularly necessary for the effective ministry and outreach of the church. For this reason we will call them *ministry gifts*.

A BIBLICAL VIEW OF MINISTRY GIFTS

Ministry gifts are spiritual graces expressed specifically for the edification, exhortation, and unity of the body of Christ and its outreach. They may not seem like supernatural gifts, but they are. Exercised by the Holy Spirit, these spiritual gifts go far beyond the reach of natural talent or ability. Let's look closely at each gift and examine how it is used in the church.

Prophecy. To *prophesy* means "to foretell, or to forthtell under inspiration." Instructions for the ministry of prophesying is given in 1 Corinthians 14. A Christian should seek to prophesy (v. 1). One who prophesies speaks to people, not to God (v. 3).

The content of a true message of prophecy is always "edification and exhortation and comfort" (v. 3, *NKJV*). Prophecy edifies the church (v. 4). A word of prophecy is for believers, not for unbelievers (v. 22). Yet, unbelievers may be convicted and get saved as a result of prophesying (vv. 24, 25).

Finally, prophesying should always be according to the prophet's faith (Romans 12:6).

Serving (ministry, helps). The Greek word used in Romans 12:7, *diakonia*, is the same word used elsewhere in the New Testament for the ministry of the deacon (Acts 6:2-4). This word was also used for the preparation of food and for other types of spiritual service, including the ministry of reconciliation (2 Corinthians 5:18).

In the New Testament, the office of a deacon was very important. Deacons monitored the money tables, or cash funds (Acts 6:2), and oversaw the ministry of the widows, the poor, and the sick. This gift is not limited to a church position, but every church needs servant leaders. As a pastor, I have seen a lot of people put in ministry positions because of popularity or social prestige. Inevitably, these leaders, though well-intentioned, wreak havoc on a church or a ministry of the church.

When looking for those to lead us in ministry, it is important to look for those with the gift of serving. Servant leadership is a key to successful ministry in every church. God does not require graduate degrees, wealth, or talent. He requires a servant heart that is available and pliable. The supernatural power of the Holy Spirit can use the gift of ministry only through those who have a servant's heart.

"This is the one I esteem: he who is humble and contrite in spirit, and trembles at my word" (Isaiah 66:2).*

"Whoever wants to become great among you must be your servant, and whoever wants to be first must be your slave—just as the Son of Man did not come to be served, but to serve, and to give his life as a ransom for many" (Matthew 20:26-28).

A man dreamed that he was allowed to go to heaven and hell. In hell he was taken to a room with a large pot of stew in the middle. The stew smelled delicious, but all around the pot were people starving, desperate. The spoons they held in their hands had unusually long handles which reached all the way to the pot; but because the spoon handles were longer than their arms, they were unable to return the spoons of stew to their mouths. Their suffering was terrible and continuous.

Heaven was identical to hell in his dream. The rooms were identical, the pot of stew in the middle of the room was the same, and the spoons were the same. But the people in the room were well-fed and joyous. The man noticed that the people in this room were feeding each other. This is a perfect illustration of the gift of serving. The church needs people with the Spirit-anointed ability to serve others and find personal fulfillment in doing so. The effectiveness of the church as a ministry body depends largely on those who will operate in this critical area of spiritual giftedness.

Teaching. Peter's Sunday school teacher finished telling her class the story of Jonah and the whale. She decided to quiz the children on their memory of the lesson. She asked, "Peter, what is the moral of this lesson?" Peter thought for a minute, then said, "People make whales throw up!" Teachers have to be as creative as the kids. One Sunday school teacher sent a note home with one of her junior boys. It noted that the young student was "very adept in the creative use of visual aids for learning." When the boy's father called for an interpretation, the teacher explained, "It means he copies from the kid in the next seat."

The gift of teaching is not just about creativity, however; nor is it just about Sunday school teachers. Ephesians 4:11 associates this gift with pastors. From the pastor's pulpit to the Sunday school teacher's podium, every church needs teachers who exercise the gift of teaching. There is a difference between gifted teachers and teachers with "the gift." A lot of people can teach, and some are very good at it. But the individual used by the Holy Spirit to teach is able to supernaturally communicate the truth of God's Word to people's lives with the anointing of God.

I have often left the class feeling the material I received was informative and helpful. The teacher may have even been creative in communicating effectively. At other times I have sat under the teaching of someone who was endowed with the gift of teaching. The lesson touched not only my head but my heart. Fresh revelation challenged and transformed me as my spirit received God's message. Sometimes the Holy Spirit spoke directly through the teacher and gave me answers to things I had prayed about for weeks. That's the gift of teaching at work!

Believers whom God uses with this gift area are by no means exempt from study or preparation. While it is true that the Holy Spirit is our teacher (John 14:17, 26), and that He will teach us directly (Jeremiah 31:34; John 6:45; 2 Corinthians 3:3; 1 John 2:20, 27), Jesus said that the Holy Spirit would "remind you of everything I have said to you" (John 14:26). This implies that we need to know what Jesus said; we need to know the Word.

All week a pastor kept telling himself, "Perhaps the Holy Spirit will tell me what to say on Sunday morning." Sunday came, and he stood before his congregation unprepared. When he asked the Holy Spirit what to tell the congregation, a heavenly voice said, "Tell the people you are unprepared!"

Imagine the difference in our churches if all of our teachers had the gift of teaching! The entire body of Christ would be transformed by the Word of God. The gift of teaching in operation can make it happen. I encourage all teachers to begin praying that God would use you in the *gift* of teaching, not just in the *position* of teacher.

Exhorting (encouraging). Martin Luther said, "Teaching and exhortation differ from each other in . . . that teaching is directed to the ignorant, but exhortation to those who have knowledge." Being "in Christ" does not mean we don't have problems or need encouraging. As a pastor I have seen as many Christians suffer from depression and lack of motivation as I have non-Christians. An anonymous writer quipped, "Even if you are on the right track, you'll get run over if you just sit there."

Praise God for those in the church with the gift of exhortation. They include the preacher who comes to the pulpit with a fresh word of hope to raise you above your problems. The exhorter needs no pulpit, however. He or she may be the person sitting beside you in the pew.

Richard Halverson tells the story of the frog who fell into a pothole and couldn't get out. His friends couldn't get him to muster enough strength to jump out of the pothole, so they gave up and left him to his fate. The next day they saw him bounding around just fine and asked him how he did it. "We thought you couldn't get out," they said.

"I couldn't, but a truck came along and I had to," the frog replied.

Exhorters are like that truck—God uses them to motivate you and give you hope. We need more exhorters in our churches.

The Greek word for *exhortation* (KJV) is *paraklesis*, meaning "to exhort, comfort, to call near, to summon for help." In John 14:16, the Holy Spirit is called the "Comforter" (KJV); the Greek word is *Parakletos*, "the One summoned or called to one's side for aid." We can count on the Holy Spirit to come to our aid in time of need and speak peace to our minds and hope to our souls. The people in the body of Christ that God uses for this needed ministry exercise the gift of exhortation.

Many people come into our churches hurt, wounded, discouraged, and hopeless. God help us to allow the gift of exhortation to flow through us to reach hurting people. This gift has no special skill requirements, just people who want God to use them to be a supernatural blessing in someone's life.

Giving. While the gift of exhortation meets the spiritual and emotional needs of individuals, the gift of giving helps meet the physical needs of others. The Greek word used here is *metadidomi*, which means "to impart, to share, to give." It relates to sharing material aid to those in need.

Scriptural examples of the use of this gift includes Barnabas, who sold his land and gave the money to meet the needs of the early church (Acts 4:36, 37). Believers sold their personal possessions to meet the needs of the body (2:44, 45; 4:34, 35). It is interesting to note that each of these examples of the gift of giving came immediately after an out-pouring of the Holy Spirit. Giving should be a part of our worship. Taking an offering "when the Spirit is moving" upon the congregation is not out of order—it is Scriptural. Some of the best offerings our church has given came immediately following a move of God in the worship service where the gifts of the Spirit were flowing in liberty.

This gift is not limited to just the wealthy, or those who have a lot of material goods to share. In Ephesians 4:28, Paul used the same Greek word *(metadidomi)* to encourage the poor to work in order that they might be able to let God use them in this gift of giving. Mark Tidd of Webster, New York, describes an experience from his college days:

An old man showed up at the back door of the house we were rent-ing. Opening the door a few inches, we saw glassy eyes set in a furrowed face glistening with silver stubble. He clutched a wicker basket holding a few unappealing vegetables. He bid us good morning and offered his produce for sale. We made a quick pur-chase to alleviate both our pity and our fear.

To our chagrin, he returned the next week, introducing himself as Mr. Roth, the man who lived in the little shack down the road. As our fears subsided, we got close enough to realize it wasn't alco-hol but cataracts that marbleized his eyes. On subsequent visits, he would shuffle in, wearing two mismatched right shoes, and pull out a harmonica. With glazed eyes set on future glory, he'd puff out old gospel tunes between conversations about vegetables and reli-gion.

On one visit, he exclaimed, "The Lord is so good! I came out of my shack this morning and found a bag full of shoes and clothing on my porch."

"That's wonderful, Mr. Roth!" we said. "We're happy for you."
"You know what's even more wonderful?" he asked. "Just yester-day I met some people who could really use them."

How productive our ministry of giving will be if church members are encouraged to seek the Lord for the gift of giving. Much joy and satisfaction comes from this gift. Jesus said, "It is more blessed to give than to receive" (Acts 20:35). This gift should be sought by all

Spirit-filled believers because it is just as much of a blessing to the one who uses the gift as it is to the giver.

Leadership (ruling, governing). This gift has to do with the oversight of something. The Greek word, *proistemi*, means "to set over, to rule." This word is also used to show concern or caring for people. Leaders are needed in each church to oversee particular ministries or groups of people with a heart for caring for them. The King James Version translates this word as "ruleth." In our society today, the word *ruling* often speaks to us of a dominating, or tyrant, type of leadership. That meaning is far from the meaning of this gift. Those with the gift of leadership lead with humility and a servant's heart. They do not use the gift to be a dictator but to be a better servant.

I am glad that this gift is listed in Scripture for us because some churches are not in short supply of people who want to "run the show." A veteran politician was trying to explain to a newly elected one how it is in Washington, D.C., when an old, rotten, deteriorating log floated down the Potomac River. "This city is like that log," the older politician said.

"How's that?"

"Well, there are probably over 100,000 grubs, ants, bugs, and critters on that old log as it floats down the river. And I imagine every one of them thinks he's steering it."

One way to assure that the right person is in charge of the right ministry is to seek God's wisdom in our choice of leaders in the church. Those used of God in the gift of leadership will be evident. They will love people, have an ability to share vision, walk in the boldness of the Spirit, and truly care for the ministry they are serving.

Acts of mercy (showing mercy). This has to do with the personal care of the needy, the sick, the hungry, the prisoners, and those without sufficient clothing. The Greek word is used in two ways in the New Testament. First, it describes God's mercy toward humanity in bestowing salvation, adoption, and blessings on mankind. Second, this gift displays God's mercy working through us to other people.

In Acts 9:36-39, we read that Dorcas cheerfully made coats and garments for widows. The grief expressed by these widows after Dorcas' death is evidence that her ministry to them involved more than just giving coats. The gift of mercy is giving accompanied by compassion and joy.

The difference between being merciful and having the gift of mercy is the attitude and the way in which an act is done. Those who exercise this gift are not concerned about the cost of their act. Their concern is foremost for the benefit of the individual they are ministering to, whether the need is financial, physical, mental, or spiritual.

A lot of people in the church can care for the needy, but only those supernaturally endowed with the gift of mercy can do so day in and day out, and keep their compassion and ability to look beyond the faults of those they are ministering to. This was the example of Christ, who gave Himself for us although we did not deserve His mercy.

A BIBLICAL ATTITUDE TOWARD MINISTRY GIFTS

Having the gifts operating in our church is not enough. The attitudes of those exercising the gifts must reflect the character of Christ for the gifts to be effective. Warren Wiersbe said, "Spiritual gifts are tools to build with, not toys to play with or weapons to fight with." It is possible to use spiritual gifts in unspiritual ways. It is for this reason that Paul concluded his exposition on ministry gifts by reminding us of three attitudes that are critical to the successful operation of the gifts in the church (Romans 12:9-16).

Love. Wiersbe quotes Jonathan Swift, "We have just enough religion to make us hate, but not enough to make us love one another." The purpose of the gifts is to build up the body of Christ, but without love even the supernatural gifts of the Spirit will not produce fruit effectively in the church. In Romans 12, Paul tells us that this love should be sincere (v. 9) and affectionate (v. 10).

Love is the gift of gifts. Every Spirit-filled believer should "eagerly desire spiritual gifts," but follow "the way of love" (1 Corinthians 14:1). When love is our foundation, we will "cling to what is good," (Romans 12:9), "honor one another above [ourselves]" (v. 10), "keep [our] spiritual fervor" (v. 11), "be joyful in hope, patient in affliction, faithful in prayer" (v. 12). Every believer seeking after spiritual gifts should read 1 Corinthians 13. The principles of love shared here are a perfect guide for the use of ministry gifts.

Unity. In my early ministry I served as a youth pastor under Pastor Walter Bateman. In preaching from Paul's analogy of body parts in 1 Corinthians 12:12-26, he said, "Why did God not put our eyeballs on our fingertips? This way we could look over, under, around, and behind things with only the help of a bent knuckle and compliant wrist." His argument seemed quite rational until he held up his fingernail for which had recently been smashed by a hammer. The visual aid was graphic.

God placed the parts of the body where they would be most effective, and the same applies to the gifts of the Spirit. There are a diversity of gifts, but, like our body parts, each gift is equally necessary to bring unity and to make the body complete and functional. Those used by God in ministry gifts must remember that they are only a part of the whole. How we use the gifts are as important as what we do. Paul said in Romans 12:16, "Live in harmony with one another." Remembering our God-given place in the body allows us to minister in unity.

Humility. "Do not be proud, but be willing to associate with people of low position" (Romans 12:16). A lot of good-intentioned believers seek after the more demonstrative "power gifts," such as healing and miracles. The ministry gifts are often overlooked because they are used and served in humility, and are often unnoticed by the crowds.

In *Waking From the American Dream*, Don McCullough writes:

> During the war, England needed to increase its production of coal. Winston Churchill called together labor leaders to enlist their support. At the end of his presentation he asked them to picture in their minds a parade which he knew would be held in Picadilly Circus after the war. First, he said, would come the sailors who kept the vital sea lanes open. Then would come the soldiers who had come home from Dunkirk and then gone to defeat Rommel in Africa. Then would come the pilots who had driven the Luftwaffe from the sky.
>
> Last of all, he said, would come a long line of sweat-stained, soot-streaked men in miner's caps. Someone would cry from the crowd, "And where were you during the critical days of our struggle?" And from 10,000 throats would come the answer, "We were deep in the earth with our faces to the coal."

Not all the gifts of the Spirit are prominent or glamorous. But those used by God in ministry gifts are "clutch players" on the team. Like the coal miners were to the operation of the war, so the ministry gifts are to the operation of the church. They rally the church to victory time after time. Without the ministry gifts in operation, our churches easily become a social gathering place for the "chosen." God has placed these gifts in the church to enable the church to minister to every age group, social class, race, language, and gender.

CONCLUSION

Ephesians 3:20 tells us that God wants to "do immeasurably more than all we ask or imagine, according to his power that is at work within us." God wants to expand your ministry potential by the supernatural power of His Holy Spirit. Are you willing to do more for God? Do you want God to use you? Ask God today to fill you with His precious Holy Spirit and use you in these rewarding ministry gifts. You will be blessed and so will your church.

*Scriptures are from the *New International Version* unless otherwise indicated.

QUESTIONS

For Thought:

1. Of the seven ministry gifts listed in Romans 12:6-8, which do you think fits your aptitude and abilities the most?
2. Do you feel God has placed a gift in you to serve the body?
3. Despite the current emphasis on gifts, why do you think the writer said, Having the gifts operating in the church is not enough?"
4. Think of ways in which you can promote unity in the church.

For Discussion:

1. What are some of the reasons you think the writer called love "the gift of gifts?"
2. Share with the group testimonials of someone who exhibited the true gift of mercy.

ACTIVITIES

1. Show appreciation in both words and actions for the servant-leaders in your church.
2. Do an act of kindness for someone without letting him see you. (This act will exhibit the quality of humility.)

Chapter 9

THE HOLY SPIRIT AND DISCIPLESHIP

A disciple follows his mentor. Not only is Jesus our mentor, but so in the Holy Spirit. What role does the Holy Spirit have in making us disciples?

THE HOLY SPIRIT AND DISCIPLESHIP

by
Daniel L. Black

Scripture: Luke 14:25-27

INTRODUCTION

Christian discipleship requires a level of commitment to Jesus Christ that we are not capable of giving by our own strength and determination. A disciple is a follower, but being a disciple of Jesus Christ is more than following. Christian discipleship requires an identification with and a self-denying loyalty to Christ that goes beyond merely following Him.

Greek philosophers, such as Socrates, Plato, and Aristotle, had their disciples. These disciples accepted the teachings and imitated the ways of their teachers, but they were never committed to their teachers the way Christian disciples are committed to Christ. In the time of Jesus, John the Baptist had disciples (Matthew 9:14) and so did the Pharisees (22:16). Jewish religious leaders called themselves disciples of Moses (John 9:28). But discipleship in these groups did not approach what it means to be a disciple of Jesus Christ.

For the Christian, Jesus Christ is not just a respected teacher and example; He is believed in and reverenced as God. He is worshiped and obeyed as Savior, Lord, and Master. The Christian disciple does not merely follow Christ, he belongs to Christ. This kind of discipleship commitment requires more than human resolve. It requires the help of the Holy Spirit.

Since Christian discipleship means belief in and obedience to Christ as Lord and God, we must have the help of the Holy Spirit. No person can truthfully confess that Jesus Christ is Lord and submit to His lordship without spiritual enlightenment and the enabling of the Holy Spirit (1 Corinthians 12:3). To be disciples of Jesus Christ, we must submit to the sanctifying work of the Holy Spirit, the teaching of the Holy Spirit, and the guidance of the Holy Spirit.

DISCIPLESHIP AND SANCTIFICATION BY THE HOLY SPIRIT

To be disciples of Jesus Christ, we need the sanctifying work of the Holy Spirit in our lives. Christian baptism is a public testimony of faith in Jesus Christ as our personal Savior and Lord. It also means we will continue to prove our faith in Christ by obedience to Him; and obedience is discipleship. Obedience to Jesus Christ is the practical goal of the sanctifying work of the Holy Spirit in our lives.

Obedience to Christ is not only doing but also being. As Christians we are called not only to imitate His good deeds, we are also called to be like Him. If we do the kind of deeds Jesus did but fail to have His attitude and character, we are not obeying Him and we are not His disciples.

The sanctifying work of the Holy Spirit in our lives is to bring us into obedience to Jesus Christ. Without this work of the Spirit, bringing us into conformity to the character and will of Christ, we cannot be His disciples. In a letter to the church at large, the apostle Peter said believers are *sanctified by the Holy Spirit to obey Jesus Christ* (1 Peter 1:2).

There is an implicit understanding among Christians that sanctification is a work of the Holy Spirit. Christian discipleship is dependent on the sanctifying work of the Holy Spirit. *The Encyclopedia of Religion and Ethics* gives this almost universally accepted (among Christians) definition of *sanctification*:

> In general, sanctification is the work of the Holy Spirit of God, in delivering men from the guilt and power of sin, in consecrating them to the service and love of God, and in imparting to them,

initially and progressively, the fruits of Christ's redemption and the graces of a holy life.

Real discipleship is holy living. Obedience to Jesus Christ is not just a matter of doing good deeds on our own initiative. *Obedience to Jesus Christ—real discipleship—is holy living;* and holy living is only possible as the Holy Spirit delivers us from the power of sin and imparts to us the graces of the holy life.

On the evening before His death, Jesus talked to the 12 disciples about abiding in Him and being spiritually fruitful. He summed up His discourse by saying, "Herein is my Father glorified, that ye bear much fruit; so shall ye be my disciples" (John 15:8). What is the "much fruit" that is proof of Christian discipleship? It is apparent from all Jesus said about this that Christian discipleship requires us to manifest the love of Christ, be possessed of His character, and do His works.

When Jesus called people to be His disciples, He required that their devotion to Him be the same devotion given to God. The God of Israel had commanded that people love Him with all their heart, soul, mind, and strength. Jesus commands that we love Him more than we love father, mother, spouse, or children.

In effect, Jesus says: *If you would be My disciple, I must be first in your life. Your commitment to Me must take priority over all other commitments.* This is no easy discipleship.

When we come to Christ to save us and deliver us from the power and guilt of sin, it is in response to the convincing work of the Holy Spirit. As saved people, every time we respond to Christ's call to discipleship by actually putting Him first, that decision is made possible by the sanctifying work of the Holy Spirit in our lives. *That level of commitment to Christ is made possible "through sanctification of the Spirit, unto obedience"* (1 Peter 1:2).

DISCIPLESHIP AND THE TEACHING OF THE HOLY SPIRIT

To be disciples of Jesus Christ, we need the teaching of the Holy Spirit regarding Christ. The classical understanding of discipleship always supposes the model of a teacher-pupil relationship, with the pupil, of course, being the disciple of the teacher. This was the pattern with the Greek philosophers and their disciples, the Pharisees and their disciples,

John the Baptist and his disciples, and Jesus and His disciples. The disciple must have knowledge of what is required to be a disciple. The disciple needs to be taught. The disciple needs to learn.

Jesus was a teacher. He was constantly teaching His disciples, even to the last night before His death. After His resurrection, He continued to teach the disciples until the day of His ascension, and expounded "unto them in all the scriptures the things concerning himself" (Luke 24:27). "Then opened he their understanding, that they might understand the scriptures" (v. 45). During this time, He spoke to them "of the things pertaining to the kingdom of God" (Acts 1:3).

There can be no discipleship without teaching and learning. To be disciples of Christ we must be taught by Him and learn of Him. We have to know His words, deeds, and character. We have to know not only His commandments but also His example. We have to know not only His deeds but also His attitude. But how can we learn these things we need to know for discipleship? Jesus Christ is no longer present in body to teach us as He taught the 12 apostles so long ago. How are we to prepare ourselves for discipleship?

Jesus acknowledged to His disciples that He would not always be present in body to teach them. But to compensate for this loss of His physical presence, He promised to send the Holy Spirit: "I will pray the Father, and he shall give you another Comforter, that he may abide with you for ever. . . . *The Comforter, which is the Holy Ghost, whom the Father will send in my name, he shall teach you all things,* and bring all things to your remembrance, whatsoever I have said unto you" (John 14:16, 26).

The apostle Paul, writing to the Corinthians, shed additional light on the teaching ministry of the Holy Spirit in relation to Christian discipleship: "We speak, not in the words which man's wisdom teacheth, but which the Holy Ghost teacheth; comparing spiritual things with spiritual. But the natural man receiveth not the things of the Spirit of God. . . . But we have the mind of Christ" (1 Corinthians 2:13, 14, 16).

There is a spiritual dimension of Christian discipleship that does not exist in other kinds of discipleship. For example, many people in the Western world have been, and still are, the disciples of Plato. The teachings of this Greek philosopher are regarded by historians as foundational to much of what we call "Western civilization." Suppose I wanted to become a disciple of Plato. Since he died 340 years before Jesus was born, it would not be possible for me to learn directly from Plato himself. Instead, I would have to read his writings and learn all I could about him from what others have said about him. Then, with this knowledge in mind, I could try to be a follower (a disciple) of Plato. This process is somewhat like, though much unlike, what is involved in becoming a disciple of Jesus Christ. However, the spiritual dimension would be missing.

By way of comparison, suppose I set out to become a disciple of Jesus Christ. First, I must reckon with the fact that Jesus Christ died for my sins, but He did not remain dead. God raised Him from the dead, and He is alive forever. He is not physically present (as Plato isn't), but He is alive and spiritually present. Nevertheless, to learn about Jesus I need to read or hear what the Bible says about Him. It will even be helpful to hear about Him from others who are already His disciples. But without the teaching of the Holy Spirit, none of this will make me a disciple of Jesus Christ. This is very different from deciding to be a follower of Plato. There is a spiritual dimension to being a disciple of Jesus Christ, and this spiritual dimension can be introduced only by the Holy Spirit.

The Holy Spirit enlightens and convinces by teaching. I cannot believe, understand, or respond to what the Bible and others say about Christ except as the Holy Spirit enlightens and convinces me by His teaching. Christian discipleship requires faith—sincere belief—that Jesus died for my sins and rose from the dead to give me life. But I will not believe this except as the Holy Spirit teaches me and convinces me it is true. Christian discipleship requires personal involvement with Jesus Christ—commitment to Him as my personal Savior and Lord. But I will not make this commitment except as the Holy Spirit teaches me and convinces me that I should. This spiritual dimension of Christian discipleship is missing from all other models of discipleship.

The Holy Spirit is a teacher like Jesus. After our initial introduction into Christian discipleship, we continue to need the Holy Spirit as teacher. The fact is that Christ is present through the Spirit to teach us all we need to know from the Scriptures to be His disciples. When Jesus promised to send the Holy Spirit, He said, "I will come to you" (John 14:18)—meaning that He would come to us in the person of the Holy Spirit to be our teacher. As we read and study the Bible, and as we hear it preached and taught, the Spirit of Christ (the Holy Spirit) is present to give us the spiritual knowledge and understanding we need to be His disciples.

DISCIPLESHIP AND THE GUIDANCE OF THE HOLY SPIRIT

We need the guidance of the Spirit for discipleship. To be disciples of Jesus Christ, we need the guidance of the Holy Spirit to fulfill the call of Christ. Every disciple of Christ is called to live by the principles, commandments, and example of Christ found in the Bible. This call to discipleship is the same for every person. But individually, every person does not fulfill the call to discipleship in the same way. In addition to the general call to discipleship found in Scripture, every believer in Christ receives a particular call to discipleship that will lead him to serve Christ in ways different from other disciples.

There are distinctions between the general and particular calls to discipleship. The distinction between the general call to discipleship and particular calls to discipleship is most apparent in those who are called to serve as pastors, missionaries, evangelists, or teachers. For example, the missionary has received a general call to discipleship, but he or she has also received a particular call to fulfill the call to discipleship primarily by doing the work of a missionary. This same principle of general and particular calls to discipleship applies to every Christian, although it may be much less conspicuous in those who do not have prominent roles of leadership in the church.

Jesus said to His disciples, "When he, the Spirit of truth, is come, he will guide you into all truth . . . and he will shew you things to come. He shall glorify me" (John 16:13, 14). On another occasion, Jesus had said, "If ye continue in My word, then are ye my disciples indeed; and ye shall know the truth, and the truth shall make you free" (8:31, 32). *These statements of Jesus show a close relationship between discipleship, knowing and living by the truth, and the guidance of the Holy Spirit.*

Jesus acknowledged and appreciated the individual uniqueness of His disciples. He gave them guidance in truth for obeying the general call to discipleship and for fulfilling their particular calls to discipleship.

The Spirit guides in the general call to discipleship. Today, the Holy Spirit works in the same way to give guidance for discipleship. Before we can fulfill our particular calls to discipleship, we are faced every day with the challenge of simply being Christians—the challenge of obeying the general call to discipleship. For this the Holy Spirit is always present, exerting His influence on our minds and hearts that we may know and live by the truth for the glory of Christ.

The Holy Spirit is also present to give us guidance in fulfilling our particular calls to discipleship. The Holy Spirit helps us know where we need to be and what we need to do to fulfill our particular call to discipleship. We see this in Christians persuaded by the Holy Spirit that they must minister in a certain place, to a specific person or group, and in some definite way. Thus it is that Christians "feel" called of God to go here or there and to minister in different ways. *And thus it is that all the discipleship work of the church gets done—under the guidance of the Holy Spirit, in keeping with the truth revealed in Scripture, and for the glory of Jesus Christ.*

CONCLUSION

Becoming a Christian can be likened to becoming a member of an organization where the membership fee is nothing and the dues are everything. The membership fee is nothing because Christ paid the price for our redemption and inclusion in the church. But the dues are everything, for Christian discipleship demands that we withhold nothing from Christ. As the song says, His love, "so amazing, so divine, demands my soul, my life, my all."

Am I capable of giving to Christ my soul, my life, my all? No, but I have a Helper, an Enabler, the Holy Spirit of God. If I am willing, He is able. Through sanctification He will bring me into obedience to Christ. He will teach me how to give my soul, my life, my all to Christ every day. He will guide me in the way of truth to the complete fulfillment of my calling to Christian discipleship. *Am I willing to submit to the Spirit?*

QUESTIONS

For Thought:

1. What distinguishes Jesus, the teacher and example, above other teachers and philosophers?
2. For what purpose are believers sanctified (see 1 Peter 1:2)?
3. Three people or groups of people had disciples in the New Testament. Name them.
4. In what ways have you experienced the Holy Spirit guiding your life?

For Discussion:

1. Discuss 1 Corinthians 12:3.
2. What does obedience to Jesus involve?
3. We have the Bible containing the words of Jesus. Why do you think we need the Holy Spirit for guidance?
4. Discuss the general call to discipleship, and the particular call to discipleship.

ACTIVITIES

Real discipleship is holy living. In your devotions this week, renew your commitment to Christ, and look for ways to exemplify true discipleship (see Acts 4:13).

Chapter 10

THE HOLY SPIRIT AND EVANGELISM

Discuss the greatest revival you have personally experienced.

THE HOLY SPIRIT AND EVANGELISM

by
James E. Cossey

Scripture: Acts 9:1-22

INTRODUCTION

The world's most beloved evangelist, Billy Graham, was recently dismissed from the hospital after treatment for injuries he suffered in a fall. It was obvious to all that Parkinson's disease was taking its toll on this stalwart messenger of Christ.

A television reporter questioned Mr. Graham: "Sir, what are your plans for the future of your ministry?"

Without hesitation, Billy Graham, now 77, replied, "I plan to continue to preach the gospel! I have several more good years to give to the ministry!"

Evangelism is the heartbeat of God! John 3:16 tells us that God sent us His Son as an evangelist. Our Lord's most beloved apostle was called "the evangelist." Without doubt, those who have most profoundly affected the Christian faith through the centuries were Jesus himself, the apostle Peter, John, and Paul.

CHOSEN TO EVANGELIZE

The greatest evangelist of all time was perhaps the apostle Paul. Why was Paul such a powerful communicator for Christ?

Evangelism is more than a career choice. It is more than a chosen vocation. Paul, as well as anybody, knew this! Was he not committed to a different lifestyle? Didn't he know what he wanted to do with his life? But God had different plans! Paul was literally arrested by the Holy Spirit, and chosen to evangelize!

No man ever needed a Savior more than Saul of Tarsus! Saul was a rigid rejecter of Jesus, a legalistic Jew, a persecutor of the church! He was a witness to the stoning of Stephen! "As for Saul, he made havoc of the church, entering every house, and dragging off men and women, committing them to prison" (Acts 8:3).*

But that was before he encountered the risen Christ! As Saul was seeking for members of the church to persecute, the Lord of the church was seeking Saul to make him an apostle and an evangelist! Saul discovered the meaning of Jesus' words in Luke 19:10: "For the Son of Man has come to seek and to save that which was lost."

With written authority from the high priest, and with letters from the synagogues of Damascus, Saul was on a mission of murder when he met Jesus, who was on a mission of mercy! With authority to dispense death, he came face-to-face with the One who gives life!

Discipleship is a public commitment. Occasionally, we hear someone speak of secret saints or disguised disciples—those who claim a personal commitment to Christ, but have never made a public profession. Yet, the Bible is clear that discipleship is a public commitment.

Saul may have preferred a quiet conversion. After all, how would he explain his change of behavior? Perhaps he could keep it quiet for awhile, and then break it gently to his friends. But Scripture knows nothing of private conversion. Every person Jesus ever called, He called publicly. Saul of Tarsus would be no exception! He had publicly rejected Christ, he must publicly accept Him. He had publicly reviled the church, he must publicly align himself with it! Saul had no choice! Jesus called him publicly!

Can you imagine being on the examining board to consider credentials for Saul of Tarsus? Can you imagine having Saul for Sunday dinner the week after his conversion? Would you like Saul to be your overnight guest . . . to sleep down the hall from your children . . . to eat at your table?

Even saintly Ananias, chosen to baptize Saul, was skeptical and cautious, as were many early Christians! Ananias prayed, "Lord, I have heard from many about this man, how much harm he has done to Your saints in Jerusalem, And here he has authority from the chief priests to bind all who call on Your name" (Acts 9:13, 14).

God's reassurance to Ananias was, "Go, for he is a chosen vessel of Mine to bear my name before Gentiles, kings, and the children of Israel" (v. 15).

What a statement! What a commendation! "He is a chosen vessel!"

The beauty of evangelism is that God doesn't see us as we are. He sees us as we can become. He doesn't see the lost through eyes of vengeance; He sees them through eyes of love!

Sauls are all around us! No obvious potential for God or good can be seen in their lives. Their values are diametrically opposed to ours. They nauseate us. Their lifestyle is repulsive. Their vocabulary is atrocious. In everything we stand for, they stand for something else! Love them? How can we love them, when we don't even like them?

But Jesus does. He doesn't love their values, or their lifestyle, or their vocabulary. But He loves them! He loves them and He seeks them. The woods are full of potential chosen vessels, just like Saul of Tarsus who became known to us as the apostle Paul!

Can't you see the wonderful spiritual cycle God sets in motion? Ananias, an unworthy vessel, reaches Saul, another unworthy vessel— so that Saul may reach someone else, another unworthy vessel; and on the cycle goes! That's what happens when the church realizes that we are chosen to evangelize!

Jesus said, "You did not choose me, but I chose you and appointed you that you should go and bear fruit, and that your fruit should remain, that whatever you ask the father in My name He may give you" (John 15:16).

FILLED WITH POWER (Acts 9:17-19)

An enabling for engagement. It's one thing to be chosen to evangelize, it's something else to be anointed for the task. Too often God's people attempt to do God's work without God's power! The spiritual anointing to accomplish this work was as important for Saul as knowing that God had chosen him!

One of Dr. Ray H. Hughes' famous Pentecostal sermons is titled "The Anointing Makes the Difference!" That statement is more than a catchy cliché for camp meeting consumption! It's a fact! The anointing does make a difference! Somehow we need to hear again the word of the Lord that came to Zerubbabel: "'Not by might nor by power, but by My Spirit,' says the Lord of hosts" (Zechariah 4:6).

An anointing with authority. Before Saul, God's chosen vessel, could function as a chosen vessel, the anointing was a necessity! When Saul met Christ on the Damascus road, a blinding light rendered him sightless. For three days he was without sight, food, and drink.

Somehow we need to rediscover that genuine conversion is a stripping experience! Conversion to Christ didn't make Saul an immediate celebrity! Conversion to Christ didn't elevate him to the pinnacle of success! Instead, conversion to Christ stripped him of everything! It was only after Saul had been stripped, that he could be saturated with the power of God!

Three things happened when Ananias laid hands on Saul and prayed for him (Acts 9:17, 18):

- Something like scales fell off his eyes.
- Saul was baptized as a public profession of faith in Jesus Christ.
- Saul received the baptism in the Spirit, and although the passadoes not tell us that Saul spoke in tongues, we know he did because of his testimony in 1 Corinthians 14:18.

The important truth here is that Saul's scales would not have fallen off . . . Saul's baptism might not have occurred . . . his mighty teachings on the power of the Holy Spirit might never have been heard had it not been for the anointing of the Spirit that came to him through the laying on of hands by Ananias.

You and I are also chosen vessels! The seeking Savior has sought and found us! His challenge to us is that we find others! But we are impotent in our evangelism when we try to do it in the power of the flesh! The anointing breaks the yoke! The anointing brings liberty! The anointing brings deliverance! The anointing makes the difference!

An unction for usefulness. An old country preacher preached often about the unction! Constantly he advised people through his sermons that they needed the unction. A young "smart-aleck" confronted the preacher one day and asked, "What is the unction, anyway?"

The saintly servant of God never ventured as much as a smile, as he replied, "I don't rightly know if I can explain what the unction is, but I can sure tell you when the unction ain't!"

In truth, the unction is a communication gift from the Holy Spirit. The word *unction* appears but once in the Bible (1 John 2:20). In the *New King James Version*, the word is translated "anointing": "But you have an anointing from the Holy One."

The Greek word is *chrisma*, which means "anointing." The anointing is not earned, developed, cultivated, or learned. It is a gift from God in response to the yielding of His people! Without it we cannot penetrate the hardness of men's hearts! Without it we cannot melt the spirits of the lost! Without the anointing of the Holy Spirit, we cannot be chosen vessels for the glory of God!

WITNESSING IN POWER (Acts 9:20-22; 13:1-12)

Expressive power. What was the first thing Saul did after the anointing of the Spirit? He began immediately to witness to others about what Christ had done in his life! The key word is *immediately*. "Immediately he preached Christ in the synagogues, that He is the Son of God" (Acts 9:20).

And what was the reaction of the people who heard him? "Then all who heard were amazed" (v. 21). They said, "This is the one who persecuted the church in Jerusalem! This is the one who came here to persecute the Christians! What in the world has happened to Saul?" Their questions merely fueled Saul's flame. "But Saul increased all the more in strength, and confounded the Jews who dwelt in Damascus, proving that this Jesus is the Christ" (v. 22).

Progressive power. Isn't it amazing to see the progression of God's blessing on Saul? At the beginning of chapter 9, he is breathing out threats and murder against the disciples of the Lord. On the Damascus road he falls to the ground in the presence of the resurrected Christ, and says, "Who are you, Lord?" (v. 5). Then he received Christ, was baptized, and started preaching! Almost immediately, he began to confound the Jews and, through his anointed instruction, actually proved to them that Jesus is the Christ, the Son of God!

At Jerusalem, the focal point of church-house chatter was about how Saul had preached the gospel with boldness at Damascus! God changed Saul's name to *Paul*, which means "little man." He may have been small in stature, but being chosen of God and anointed by the Spirit made him a giant in the kingdom of God!

Impressive power. The true test of the anointing comes not in the church, but in the face of the devil! The true test of evangelism is when the evangelist meets Satan eyeball-to-eyeball! It's then that we had better be sure that we are called, chosen, and anointed!

In Acts 13, Paul met Elymas the sorcerer who withstood Paul to his face. Paul, the evangelist, replied, "No problem!" Full of the Holy Spirit, Paul looked this demon-possessed man squarely in the eye, and said, "O full of all deceit and all fraud, you son of the devil, you enemy of all righteousness, will you not cease perverting the straight ways of the Lord? And now, indeed the hand of the Lord is upon you; and you shall be blind, not seeing the sun for a time" (vv. 9-11). Verse 11 continues, "And immediately a dark mist fell on him, and he went around seeking someone to lead him by the hand."

What happened? People believed when they saw what Paul had done! The proconsul, Sergius Paulus, "an intelligent man," believed the gospel when he saw Paul withstand the devil and not give ground (v. 12).

What made Paul's witness so effective? Was it what he said? Yes, it was, but it was more. What made his witness so effective was how he said what he said, and the spirit that emanated from this man of God!

CONCLUSION

Sometimes I think we've missed the mark. We place so much emphasis on education, and rightly so; we must have an educated clergy. We place a great deal of emphasis on communicative skills, and we should; we must have skilled communicators.

We emphasize homiletics and proper exegesis of Scripture. We encourage expository preaching, and we should. The need of the hour is for the preaching of the Word of God!

But the greatest witness is the believer who mirrors the Christlife every day! The greatest preacher or teacher is the one who walks what he talks. The greatest evangelist is the one who can meet the devil on his own territory, stare him in the eye, and tell it like it is!

God send us an awakening! Send a renewal to the church that will call us once again to lifestyle evangelism. Call us to a lifestyle of living the gospel as chosen vessels, searching for other chosen vessels to be enlisted into the work of the Kingdom of God!

*Scriptures are from the *New King James Version.*

QUESTIONS

For Thought:

1. What do you think of when the words "evangelize" or "evangelism" are mentioned?
2. Meditate on a particular time in your life when you were anointed for a particular task or opportunity.
3. Do you think you have been "chosen" to share the Gospel to someone? Who? How can you do it?
4. The most effective evangelist is he or she who "mirrors the Christlife every day," the writer says. Think of ways to evangelize your world better.

For Discussion:

1. Discuss the attributes of Paul that made him an ideal evangelist.
2. The writer uses the term "chosen to evangelize" in a prominent way. Discuss this thought, along with the idea that "every Christian must witness."
3. Discuss the role of the "anointing of the Holy Spirit" in evangelism.
4. In his evangelistic efforts, Paul had a confrontation with Elymas in Acts 13. Does this account have any implications for us today? What are they?

ACTIVITIES

1. Every Christian is commanded to witness. List three individuals you will endeavor to witness to this week.
2. Spend time every day praying for your church's witnessing efforts this week.

Chapter 11

WORSHIPING IN SPIRIT AND TRUTH

1. In your opinion, what do you do in worship in your church that is effective?
2. In your opinion, what do you do that is not effective?

WORSHIPING IN SPIRIT AND TRUTH

by
Samuel D. Adkerson

Scripture: Acts 2:42-47

INTRODUCTION

God has created within each individual the capacity to worship. Throughout the centuries man has instinctively reached to embrace an authority, a power, or a person beyond himself. In the Old Testament, the Philistines worshiped Dagon, the Moabites and Midianites worshiped Baal-Peor, the Babylonians worshiped Ishtar, and the Zidonians and Phoenicians worshiped Ashtoreth.

In the New Testament, the Iconians worshiped Jupiter and Mercury. In fact, they thought Barnabas and Paul were manifestations of Jupiter and Mercury in human form (Acts 14:12). The Greeks were polytheistic, and filled Mars' Hill with statues to their deities.

Men today still have their gods—Buddha, Muhammad, Confucius, and a host of others. They worship in their own way, at the designated time and place. But the only true Deity, the only One worthy of our worship, is Jehovah God, who eternally exists in three persons, namely, the Father, the Son, and the Holy Spirit. True worshipers have trusted Him for the remission of their sins and daily follow the Son as Savior and soon-coming King.

COMPONENTS OF CORPORATE WORSHIP

"We had a wonderful service. There wasn't even any preaching!" Many times this is thought to be a perfect worship service to the immature believer. But it is a mistake to place greater importance on anything other than on the Word of God. Many things in a worship service can make one feel good and even feed the soul (mind, will, and emotions); but only the Word of God can feed man's spirit. The preaching of God's Word should be the focal point of every service. All other facets of worship should prepare the believers' heart for the ingestion of the Word of God.

The altar. Altar responses should be the rule, not the exception. When believers' hearts are prepared for the Word through the worship of God in spirit and in truth and the Word of God is proclaimed with the anointing of the Holy Spirit, sinners will be saved, backsliders will be reclaimed, and believers will be sanctified and baptized in the Holy Spirit and speak with tongues as the Spirit gives the utterance. Signs and wonders will follow those who believe. Miracles will be manifested. The lame will walk; the blind will see; the weak will be made strong. Financial impossibilities will become realities, as God, the greatest financier, makes moves that even Wall Street does not understand.

Psychological and emotional problems are solved as the Holy Ghost delivers from oppression, depression, and satanic possession.

Social problems are solved as God heals relationships between husbands and wives, parents and children, siblings, and employer and employee. God placed the gifts of the Spirit in the church, and He will manifest them there when His people worship corporately. But remember, all worship must be coordinated by the Holy Spirit. No flesh shall glory in His presence. All worship must be predicated upon the Word of God.

The Sacraments. Sacraments should be a regular part of worship. Holy Communion, washing the saints' feet, and water baptism should be observed on a regular basis as part of the worship experience. The Bible says of Holy Communion, "This do in remembrance of me" (1 Corinthians 11:24). Some believers serve Communion each Sunday; others less frequently—monthly, quarterly or annually. Regardless of the frequency, Holy Communion should be an integral part of worship, since it reminds believers of what Christ did for them through His atoning death at the Cross—His body was broken and His blood was spilled that all who believe might have life and have it more abundantly.

Washing the saints' feet is a lesson in servanthood, something sorely lacking in the church as it approaches the next millennium. Jesus, just after instituting Holy Communion, poured water into a basin, girded Himself with a towel, and washed the disciples' feet. Peter at first refused to allow the Lord to wash his feet. But finally he consented because Jesus' told him it was necessary if he wanted to have a part with Christ. And Peter did not want to be ostracized from the Lord's company and ministry. Churches would have fewer problems and pastors could spend less time refereeing Christians' petty quarrels and more time spreading the gospel if washing the saints' feet was more frequently incorporated into the worship services of the church.

Water baptism—by immersion in the name of the Father and of the Son and of the Holy Ghost—should be offered to every believer as soon after conversion as practical. This does not mean, of course, that water baptism is essential to salvation. The blood of Jesus Christ does not need anything added to cleanse the sinner. Baptismal regeneration is a false doctrine predicated primarily on Acts 2:38. In this passage, baptismal regenerationists accept one and only one definition of the Greek word *eis* translated "for" in the King James Version. They construe this to mean "in order to" receive remission of sins. However, *for* has another definition as well—"because of." To illustrate: If you call your physician, complaining of a headache, and he responds by saying, "Take two aspirins *for* your headache," does he mean to take two aspirins in order to receive a headache? No! Rather, he means take two aspirins because you already have a headache, or as a result of needing relief from a headache. Likewise, one is to be baptized in water because of, or as a result of, remission of sins.

THE ELEMENTS OF CORPORATE WORSHIP

Tithes and Offerings. Believers should be given the opportunity during worship to bring to God His tithe and their offerings. This should not be viewed as an interruption of worship or as something to "get out of the way." Worship in giving should be a joyful occasion, filled with goodwill and cheer. Dedicated believers do not want to be pumped, primed, or begged to give. They simply want the opportunity and privilege to give to God. God will be pleased, and the needs of the church will be supplied.

Prayer. The psalmist said we should enter into God's presence with thanksgiving and praise (Psalm 100). In his book *The Hour That Changed the World,* Dick Eastman lists 12 types of prayer: praise (adoration), waiting, confession, scripture praying, watching, intercession, petition, thanksgiving, singing, meditation, listening, and praise (magnification). What is prayer? E.M. Bounds said, "Prayer is the contact of a living soul with God. In prayer, God stoops to kiss man, to bless man, and aid in everything that God can devise or a man can need." Charles Spurgeon said, "Prayer is the slender nerve that moves Omnipotence."

In prayer, man is given opportunity to relinquish control of every area of his life, including his problems, to God. What a privilege!

Joy and Praise. The believer who is desperate, despondent, and depressed is behind in his praise to God. He who praises God will have abundant joy, for God has promised in His Word to inhabit the praise of His people. And where God dwells, there is peace, joy, and love. Remember, the joy of the Lord is the believer's strength.

Praise is manifested in many ways: the shout, the dance, the laugh, the run, and the tears, to name a few. All of these are acceptable in God's sight, and they are all Scriptural. However, many Christians, like Samuel's mother, Hannah, praise the Lord silently, without noticeable demonstration. This too pleases God. Remember, personality differences, emotional traits, and prior teaching concerning corporate worship dictate different styles of worship. Being critical of another's worship style is judgmental, and God does not accept this behavior.

Praise may either be orchestrated or spontaneous, and both should be a part of the corporate worship service. Orchestrated praise includes the singing of choruses, psalms, hymns, and special songs selected prior to the beginning of the service. Spontaneous praise arises from the soul. Although both orchestrated and spontaneous praise are manifested by the flesh, neither should be manifested solely to gratify the flesh. All praise should glorify God, and God alone. Praise offered for the proper reason will get God's attention; and He will descend and dwell in it. The Bible is replete with admonitions to praise God; but Psalm 150:6 says it best, "Let every thing that hath breath praise the Lord."

SOME GIFTS FOR CORPORATE WORSHIP

Why did God place the gifts of the Spirit in the church? In his book

Who is the Holy Ghost? Ray H. Hughes answers, "There are, in fact, two paramount reasons for the operation of spiritual gifts. One is to glorify God, and the other is to edify the body of Christ. They are never used for self-aggrandizement or self-gratification. If God is not glorified and the church is not edified, it is not a gift of the Spirit in operation but a sinister manifestation of Satan." It might be added that Satan always speaks to man's soul through the flesh, constantly giving negative input. The gifts of the Spirit are manifested in the flesh, but they are initiated by the Holy Spirit (not by the flesh) for either the glory of God or the edification of the body of Christ.

A second question arises, "What gifts of the Spirit are available to the believer today?" For many years after my personal introduction to the Church of God in particular and to the Pentecostal Movement in general, I was taught there were nine gifts of the Spirit. In fact, I had to memorize them and their location in the Bible. I have since discovered there are many more. The best list I have found is in Paul L. Walker's book *The Ministry of Worship*, (pp. 54-59).

Motivational gifts, Romans 12:6-8. *Prophecy.* Prophecy is a divinely inspired and anointed utterance. It is a supernatural proclamation in a known language. It may operate through all who have the infilling of the Holy Spirit. The intellect, faith, and will are operative in this gift, but the exercise of it is not intellectually motivated. It is speaking forth a message from the Spirit of God.

Service (ministry). This gift enables one to minister and render loving service to meet the needs of others. It is illustrated in the work and office of the deacon (see Matthew 20:26).

Teaching. Teaching is a gift of supernatural ability to explain and apply the truths received from God for the church. The gift of teaching presupposes study and the Spirit's illumination to provide the ability to make divine truth clear to the people of God. It is distinct from the work of the prophet who spoke as the direct mouthpiece of God.

Exhortation. Exhortation literally means to call aside for the purpose of making an appeal. In a broader sense, it means to entreat, comfort, or instruct (Hebrews 10:25).

Giving. The essential meaning is to give out of a spirit of generosity. In a more technical sense, it refers to those with resources aiding those without such resources (2 Corinthians 8:2-4; 9:11-13). This gift is to be exercised without outward show or pride (Ephesians 6:5; Colossians 3:22, 23).

Leadership. This refers to the one "standing in front." It involves the exercise of the Holy Spirit in modeling, superintending, and developing the body of Christ. Leadership is to be exercised with carefulness.

Mercy. The gift of mercy means to feel sympathy with the misery of another. It is to relate to others in empathy, respect, and honesty. To be effective, this gift is to be exercised with kindness and cheerfulness—not as a matter of duty.

(Ministry gifts, 1 Corinthians 12:8-10, 28; Ephesians 4:11; 1 Peter) **4:9.** *Wisdom.* The gift of wisdom gives supernatural insight into the divine will and purpose of God. It is the power of appropriate spiritual intuition in problem-solving. It gives a sense of divine direction and enables one to be led by the Holy Spirit to act appropriately in a given set of circumstances. Wisdom is knowledge rightly applied. It works interactively with knowledge and discernment.

Faith. The gift of faith is the supernatural ability to believe God without doubt, and to combat unbelief. It is the supernatural ability to meet adverse circumstances with trust in God's messages and words. It is a joyful trust in Jesus as Messiah and Redeemer. It is an inner conviction impelled by an urgent and higher calling.

Knowledge. Knowledge may be defined as receiving information and data, and a cognitive mastery of a body of facts. The gift of knowledge is a supernatural revelation of the divine will and plan. It is knowledge of God as offered in the Word, as well as knowledge of things pertaining to God. It implies a deeper and more advanced understanding of the communicated acts of God.

Miracles. The working of miracles is the supernatural power to intervene and counteract earthly and evil forces. This gift means a literal display of power—the ability to go beyond the natural. It operates closely with the gifts of faith and healing to bring authority over sin, Satan, sickness, and the binding forces of the age.

Discernment. This gift is the supernatural power to detect the realm of the spirits and their activities. It implies the power of spiritual insight; it is the supernatural revelation of plans and purposes of the enemy and his forces.

Tongues. This gift is the supernatural utterances in a language or

Translation: word for word

languages not known to the speaker. These languages may exist in the world, or they may be unknown in the sense that they are purely a means of communication with God. They are inspired by the Holy Spirit (Isaiah 28:11; Mark 16:17; Acts 2:4; 10:44-48; 19:1-7; 1 Corinthians 12:10, 28-31; 14:2, 4-22, 26, 27-32).

Tongues serve as an evidence and sign of the indwelling and working of the Holy Spirit. *the essence of whats said*

Interpretation. The supernatural power to reveal the meaning of tongues, interpretation functions not as an operation of the mind of man, but as an operation of the mind of the Spirit. It is not translation, for the interpreter never understands the tongue he is interpreting. Rather, it is a declaration of meaning. It is exercised as a miraculous and supernatural phenomenon in the same way as the gift of speaking in tongues.

Apostleship. The apostle functions as a messenger or spokesman of God. This implies the exercise of the full spiritual power of attorney given by Christ. In apostolic days, it referred to a select group who carried out directly the ministry of Christ. In contemporary times, it refers to those with the spirit of apostleship who perform the work of the early apostles in a spiritual sense in the body of Christ.

Healing. This gift refers to supernatural healing without human aid. It does not discount the use of human instrumentation, however. Nor does it discount the use of God's creative gifts.

Helps. This means, essentially, giving help and assistance to those in need (1 Corinthians 12:28). The gift of helps actually broadens the idea beyond the work of deacons to a wider range of ministry to all who are in need—for example, the poor, the sick, the aged, orphans, and widows. The gift is a special Spirit-given ability to support, uplift, and aid others who have emotional, spiritual, and physical needs.

Evangelism. This refers primarily to a special gift of preaching or witnessing in a way that brings unbelievers into the experience of salvation. The gift of evangelism operates essentially for the establishment of new works, while pastors and teachers follow up to organize and sustain. It serves to make converts and gather them into the body of Christ, both spiritually and literally.

Pastoring. The word *pastor* comes from a root meaning "to protect," from which we get the word *shepherd.* The pastor fulfills the function of a shepherd to nurture and care for the spiritual needs of the body.

Hospitality. This word literally means "to love to do," or "to do with pleasure." Hospitality is to be employed in caring for believers and workers who visit to worship, work, and become involved in the body of Christ. In Matthew 25: 35, 40, it is illustrated in Jesus' teaching concerning judgment.

All gifts of the Spirit are resident in the believer who has received the fullness of the Spirit, as they did in the Upper Room on the Day of Pentecost. They are never possessed by the believer, but are manifested through the believer as the Spirit chooses, provided the believer is willing. Spiritual integrity must be maintained concerning the gifts of the Spirit in corporate worship. Too often, the gifts are misused and abused.

Remember, God placed the gifts of the Spirit in the church so that believers could glorify Him and edify the body of Christ.

THE UNITY OF CORPORATE WORSHIP

The elements a minister may incorporate in a worship service will differ in number for many reasons, but one thing is essential in any worship service—unity. One of Satan's greatest devices is division, and he frequently uses this tactic to thwart God's plan and purpose for those who desire to worship Him. Consequently, each believer should spend time in prayer prior to each worship service, preparing himself to receive from God or be used by God, according to His will. We cannot expect to have unity among the members of the body of Christ if the individual members are themselves not in harmony with Christ.

Believers should gather for worship with unity of purpose—to exalt the lovely name of the Lord. There is also one program, and it is outlined by Jesus in John 4:24: "God is Spirit, and those who worship Him must worship in spirit and truth" (*NKJV*). What does this mean? Each facet of the corporate worship experience should be coordinated by the Holy Ghost, and each element should be substantiated by the truth of the Word.

THE RESULTS OF CORPORATE WORSHIP

In the altar. The altar response should be the focal point of each corporate worship service. Believers should be afforded the opportunity to respond to what they have heard and to what God has convicted them to do. In his book The *Ministry of Worship*, Paul L. Walker gives some guidelines concerning altar invitations:

From the negative standpoint the altar invitation should avoid: (1) cheap psychology, (2) exaggeration, (3) humiliation of those who are in attendance, and (4) gimmicks designed to produce psychological response rather than spiritual conviction.

From the positive standpoint the altar invitation should seek: (1) to present the 'burden of the Lord' as the 'burden of the church,' (2) to involve the entire congregation in meditative, silent prayer, (3) to encourage the people to wait upon the Lord rather than demonstrate in the selfish, fleshly sense, (4) to give ample opportunity for decision, (5) to vary the method of approach, recognizing that every person may react to the gospel in a different manner, and (6) to lead seekers to Christ and the fullness of the Holy Spirit with the help of designated and trained workers.

In the Community. *First,* a reverential trust came over the people in Acts 2. They sensed that what was happening in their midst was not of man but of God. The signs and wonders were supernatural, and no one could deny it. God promised believers in every generation that these miracles would take place if worshipers would simply take Him at His Word. When God begins to manifest Himself in the church and community, people begin to take notice. They will respond positively, resulting in sinners being converted and the church gaining favor with the townspeople. Or they will respond negatively usually through persecution of some sort.

Second, praise and thanksgiving are offered as believers leave the corporate worship service to witness from house to house as they break bread and have fellowship one with another.

Third, there is a willingness to share their earthly possessions with those who are less fortunate than they are. This is always voluntary, and done during times of great need (as in first-century persecution). From all observations, this practice was restricted to the Jerusalem church. However, the twentieth-century church should also reach to those who are in need.

CONCLUSION

What gifts and ministries are available to enhance the contemporary witness? When the elements, the components, the gifts, and the unity are all properly in place for God's people, true spiritual worship results.

Worship becomes a privilege rather than a program to be conducted. It is a joy rather than a religious "jangling." Such worship is truly experienced in spirit and in truth. It glorifies and honors God, while uplifting and strengthening the worshipers.

QUESTIONS

For Thought:

1. Think of a recent service in which you worshiped "in spirit and in truth." What elements mentioned in this chapter were present in that service?

2. Which two motivational gifts would you feel most comfortable exercising, if you were anointed to do so by the Holy Spirit?

3. List some things you can do to enhance corporate worship in your church.

For Discussion:

1. Share with the group at least one outstanding "work of God" you've seen happen at the altar recently.

2. Discuss the sacraments and their regularity in your church.

3. Discuss the function of joy and praise in corporate worship.

4. What can Christians do to ensure that the ministry gifts are operating in the church?

ACTIVITIES

1. Write down, for your eyes only, three ministry gifts you would like for God to use through you in corporate worship.

2. Paul said, to "stir up the gift of God" in you, because God has not given you a spirit of fear (see Timothy 1:6, 7).

3. Ask God to help you to use your gift.

Chapter 12

THE SPIRITUAL CHURCH

Is there a difference in judging someone and being a "fruit inspector"? Explain.

THE SPIRITUAL CHURCH

by
T. David Sustar

Scripture: Galatians 5:22-26

INTRODUCTION

What is the criteria by which we judge spirituality? Some years ago, I watched as a group of people left the Church of God to begin their own church. They felt that they were too "spiritual" for the rest of us. They called their new church "The Fruit Inspectors." They would go to a church, observe it in worship, and then make a judgment as to its "spirituality."

Although most of us would never be that bold or rebellious, we have found ourselves at times looking at others to judge them. We sometimes even declare our assessment of how spiritual they are.

How do we thus judge another man's soul—that immaterial part of man which concerns life, action, and emotion? Or his spirit—that part related to worship and divine communication? The Scriptures bring us some interesting insights concerning spirituality: "But the natural man receiveth not the things of the Spirit of God: for they are foolishness unto him: neither can he know them, because they are spiritually discerned. But he that is spiritual judgeth all things, yet he himself is judged of no man" (1 Corinthians 2:14-15). It seems we can judge "things" but not one another (Matthew 7:1).

The second insight is that spiritual things are taught by the Spirit himself. This means we cannot teach spirituality as a subject, like Old Testament, or as a skill, like preaching. It must be an essential part of our being, or it is nothing at all. Spirituality is keeping in step with the Spirit. It is walking with God and growing in Christlikeness. As a popular phrase expresses it, it is "going with the flow of the Spirit."

THE BIBLICAL VIEW OF SPIRITUALITY

The greatest commandment instructs us regarding spirituality. It is total devotion to God. Its natural outgrowth is love of neighbor (Mark 12:28-34; Luke 10:25-37). It is essentially the outworking in daily life of the unity of our spirit with the Spirit of God.

There are inadequate patterns of spirituality. Lee C. Wanack, dean of academic affairs and professor of Christian Education at the Asian Theological Seminary, has written an interesting article on this subject entitled, "Rethinking Spirituality: Do Our Schools and Churches Need To Expand Their Paradigms?" It appeared in the Fall 1995 *Christian Education Journal*. Let me draw from his remarks:

There are several inadequate patterns of spirituality that need balance. First, there is the *legalistic pattern* which tries to judge spirituality by certain outward behaviors, dress, even hairstyle. Legalism lacks grace. It contrasts with the equally inadequate *libertine pattern,* which takes freedom in Christ to the extreme. The motto of this pattern is, "Sin more that grace may abound" (Romans 6:1).

The *self-denigrating pattern* focuses on personal sin and worthlessness to the exclusion of redemption. It contrasts with the inadequate opposite, the *self-affirming pattern,* that emphasizes redemption (I'm OK, you're OK) without recognition of sin.

The *pattern of privation* identifies spirituality with poverty, and the poor with the people of God. It contrasts with its opposite, the *pattern of wealth*, which identifies material wealth with the blessings of God. None of these patterns represent a balanced Christian life and should be abandoned in light of more integrated approaches that account for individual and cultural variables.

We are each His workmanship. Wanack's conclusion is noteworthy:

We need to accept wholeheartedly that there are a variety of models of spirituality, diversity of gifts, callings, roles and aptitudes. Permit people to grow according to their God-given propensities rather than foisting some pattern on them. One spiritual life can't be a Xerox copy of another. Each of us is an original creation of the Spirit of God. We are His "workmanship" (Ephesians 2:10). Diversity expressed in the unity of the body makes for a strong church. Learn from other denominations and organizations and allow for a variety of programs and activities that will foster spirituality, *but don't make them criteria to judge spirituality.* Remember *every* theology and *every* expression of spiritual life is imperfect, and we evangelicals are overdue for a dose of humility in this area. (Lee C. Wanack. "Rethinking Spirituality: Do Our Schools and Churches Need to Expand Their Paradigms?" *Christian Education Journal.* Glen Ellyn, IL: SP Ministries, Inc., Fall, 1995, p. 29f).

BEING BEFORE DOING

God is much more concerned about what we are *being* than what we are *doing*. Being always comes before doing in spiritual matters and humility; and a solemn assembly may well be necessary if we are to attain the spirituality God desires in our lives. Of course, He is concerned about our works, but the fruit will not be good if the tree is not good.

The power of the Holy Spirit cleanses from inner pollution, strengthens for service, and provides a holy love for God and one's fellows. Spirit-empowered service begins with a clean heart. Reader Harris says the apostles "needed the sin and fear burnt out, and the love and power burnt in." A.M. Hills explains, "This is what makes weak, ineffective Christians become giants. This is the blessing that enables ordinary people to do exploits and bring things to pass for God." Personal holiness commits believers to Christ's mission in the world, and holy love motivates them to joyful, effective service.

How often do we judge spirituality by non-Biblical methods, mostly by works? Some say a church is spiritual if it is active, growing, giving, winning souls, missionary-minded, smooth-running, Spirit-filled, or big. These qualities may be present in a spiritual church, but they certainly are not the Biblical criteria for a spiritual church.

Paul believed *faith, hope,* and *love* were the critical elements by which a spiritual individual and/or church would be known. In fact, these are the three principles to achieve true spirituality in a local church: "And now these three remain: faith, hope and love. But the greatest of these is love" (1 Corinthians 13:13, *NIV*). In writing to the Ephesians (1:15, 16, 18), the Colossians (1:3-6) and the Thessalonians (1 Thessalonians 1:2, 3), he illustrated this theme.

Paul enlarged his list in Galatians 5:22 to include nine fruit of the Spirit. "But the fruit of the Spirit is love, joy, peace, longsuffering, gentleness, goodness, faith, meekness, temperance: against such there is no law. And they that are Christ's have crucified the flesh with the affections and lusts. If we live in the Spirit, let us also walk in the Spirit. Let us not be desirous of vain glory, provoking one another, envying one another" (Galatians 5:22-26).

Of course, we know the fruit of the Spirit is not the only element of the Spirit-filled life which reveals true spirituality. Dr. Charles W. Conn, in his book *A Balanced Church,* states: "While the fruit of the Spirit is primary and essential to the Christian's *identification,* it is not the sole element of the church. There are other essentials as well. The fruit alone leads to *ineffectiveness* in the work of Christ. Those who exemplify only the fruit may live a Christlike *life,* but they need a further element for doing His *work.*"

He further stressed the need for three elements in the Christian experience: (1) fruit of the Spirit, (2) gifts of the Spirit, and (3) the ministry gifts.

This study focuses on the fruit of the Spirit and its results as a revelation of true spirituality in a life or a church. The truly spiritual church or life must be . . .

- In fellowship with God (love, joy, peace).
- In harmony with others (patience, gentleness, goodness).
- In witness to the world (faithfulness, meekness, temperance).

IN FELLOWSHIP WITH GOD (LOVE, JOY, PEACE)
Love is the foundation and the peak of the Christian experience. Jesus reduced the whole law and commandments to: "Thou shalt love the Lord thy God with all thy heart, and with all thy soul, and with all thy mind, and with all thy strength . . . [And] thou shalt love thy neighbour as thyself" (Mark 12:30, 31). He made it a new commandment in John

13:34, 35: "A new commandment I give unto you, That ye love one another; as I have loved you, that ye also love one another. By this shall all men know that ye are my disciples, if ye have love one to another."

This love is based on a relationship with God and is borne out in relationships with others. It is a supernatural love that is "without hypocrisy" (Romans 12:9, *NKJV*). It flows from the believer's heart without restraint because it is "shed abroad in our hearts by the Holy Ghost which is given unto us" (Romans 5:5). This is *agape* love, God's love, which does not belong primarily to the realm of the heart or to the emotions. It has most to do with behavior. It is not a matter of how we feel for others so much as how we behave toward them. If Christlike love and godly relationships are ever to become realities in our lives, we must decide to act. Believers do not react out of emotions or feelings; we act toward others as Christ acted, and acts, toward us!

Joy is not so much the pleasure of doing but the thrill of being. Joy is being reconciled to God and adopted, or received, as sons and daughters. The high and holy privilege of acceptance in the beloved is indeed a source of joy for the believer. It is "the joy of sins forgiv'n . . . the bliss the blood wash'd know . . . the peace akin to heav'n, where the healing waters flow."

This joy flows from a relationship to God which is not dependent on anything we do but simply on God's grace. Nothing on earth can give this, and nothing can take it away. There is definitely something to be said for the unmerited favor of God which flows so graciously through our lives. Knowing our sins are forgiven, that we are children of God, that we have an eternal hope in our hearts, makes us joyful.

Spiritual churches reflect the early church which greeted each other with "Joy be with you." Or they would simply say, "Rejoice" *(chairete)*. Every experience of their lives was illuminated by joy—for joy adds luster to all the Christian virtues. Paul told the Romans: "For the kingdom of God is not meat and drink; but righteousness, and peace, and joy in the Holy Ghost" (14:17).

Peace is the condition of freedom from strife internally as well as externally. The godly life of the New Testament believer was tied closely to peace, as if it were an outworking of the Spirit's inworking. "Salt is good: but if the salt have lost his saltness, wherewith will ye season it?

Have salt in yourselves, and have peace one with another" (Mark 9:50).

In His last few moments on earth, Jesus explained to His disciples how to practice the presence of God and know intimate fellowship with Him. In that last discourse He developed the basis of trust in God and the provision He had made: "But the Comforter, which is the Holy Ghost, whom the Father will send in my name, he shall teach you all things, and bring all things to your remembrance, whatsoever I have said unto you. Peace I leave with you, my peace I give unto you: not as the world giveth, give I unto you. Let not your heart be troubled, neither let it be afraid" (John 14:26, 27).

The Holy Spirit reminds us that our hearts are not to be troubled or afraid. When He, the Comforter and Counselor, comes into a life, peace also abides. For those who know the blessed Comforter, we can rejoice in the peace He brings! We understand the reality of Paul's writing to the Corinthians concerning the proper working of the gifts of the Spirit: "For God is not the author of confusion, but of peace, as in all churches of the saints" (1 Corinthians 14:33)

IN HARMONY WITH ONE ANOTHER (PATIENCE, GENTLENESS, GOODNESS)

Patience is steadfastness in obedience to God despite pressure to deny Him. It is simply suffering long. It comes out of an unwavering faith that God is sovereign and all things are under His control. While the impatient man is continually upset over injustice, over harm being inflicted or over things not going right, the Christian is not. For the Christian, patience and/or long-suffering is the result of spiritual discipline.

Many circumstances, as well as people, test our patience. Sometimes fellow Christians can create problems which try our souls. Often the testing ground is within our own homes, at work, or at school. In each trial God gives us opportunity to be an example in patience and endurance.

There is a grand assurance given in Isaiah concerning patience: "But they that wait upon the Lord shall renew their strength; they shall mount up with wings as eagles; they shall run, and not be weary; and they shall walk, and not faint" (40:31). Only the Spirit can produce such an attitude in the life of the Christian. Any person full of the Spirit will be a patient person, not given to short–temperedness. What Paul wrote will become a reality: "Be patient, bearing with one another in love" (Ephesians 4:2, *NIV*).

Gentleness is most often translated "kindness." And it has to do with our manner and attitude in dealing with our fellow man. This is the opposite of being rough, ill-mannered, hard, and unkind. If our ministry lacks tenderness and gentleness, it will also be fruitless. We will be unable to lead people to Christ. The gentle heart is the broken heart—the heart that is willing to weep over the sins of the bad as well as the sacrifices of the good.

James said, "The wisdom that is from above is first pure, then peaceable, gentle, and easy to be intreated, full of mercy and good fruits, without partiality, and without hypocrisy" (3:17).

One of the greatest needs of the church today is for kindness! So many times Christians are guilty of being short-tempered or cross with one another. This happens because one or the other has become exalted within himself and assumes the authority of Christ. However, when the fruit of the Spirit is active in the life, Christians will not reprimand each other in vengeful anger or with uncalled-for severity. In our desire to be more like our heavenly Father and our Lord Jesus, we should strive to be more gentle and kind.

Goodness has to do with love in action. It is also visiting the sick and the prisoner, giving a cup of water, feeding the hungry, clothing the needy, and so on. In truth, Christians should be more interested in giving generously than in getting. The very nature of God is giving. His children are to share His nature. God did not attempt to see how little He could give, He gave His best. In like manner we should see how much we can give, even to those who do not deserve it. When we stop to see if others merit our gift, we have missed the point of the generous goodness of this fruit of the Spirit.

Goodness speaks of our conduct toward others: "For the fruit of the Spirit is in all goodness and righteousness and truth; Proving what is acceptable unto the Lord" (Ephesians 5:9). Goodness is not only righteousness imputed but also righteousness demonstrated in everyday living. It is doing what is good out of a good heart without expecting rewards. Self has no place.

IN WITNESS TO THE WORLD (FAITHFULNESS, MEEKNESS, TEMPERANCE)

"Faithfulness" is a correct rendering of the word *faith*. We are to fasten ourselves to Christ. This begins a simple step of faith and continues with a lifelong attitude of faithfulness towards Him. Our blessed hope lies in the reliability of God. For the Christian, all fear of the present and future is erased by this thought: "God is faithful, by whom ye were called unto the fellowship of His Son Jesus Christ our Lord" (1 Corinthians 1:9). Our Father has modeled faithfulness for us so that we may understand it and in turn model it for others.

This faith is firmly founded on the Word of God. It is changless and abides forever. We live by it, and the world takes notice that we are committed to its teachings. We become witnesses as victorious believers: "This is the victory that overcometh the world, even our faith" (1 John 5:4). Even our *faithfulness.*

Meekness, contrary to present thought, has nothing to do with weakness. It is power in submission, strength under control, and authority under discipline. This combination of strength and humility is best seen in the life of Christ. In all things He had power to do things differently, yet He submitted to the will of His heavenly Father.

A godly lifestyle will be revealed from the "hidden man of the heart" through "the ornament of a meek and quiet spirit" (1 Peter 3:3, 4). This hidden man is the one the Spirit of God forms and develops in the secret workshop of the heart; namely, the new way of thinking, feeling, and willing. It flows from the life of Jesus in new spiritual life and a new nature for the believer and is adorned with the beauty of holiness (Psalm 29:2; 149:4).

Perhaps the church will soon recognize the power in meekness. Then the promise of God will be brought to pass: "If my people, which are called by my name, shall humble themselves, and pray, and seek my face, and turn from their wicked ways; then will I hear from heaven, and will forgive their sin, and will heal their land" (2 Chronicles 7:14).

Temperance is self-control, the victory over desire. Where this fruit abounds, desire will not be the dictator of our actions or our lives. Self-control implies the rational restraint of all natural impulses. It may, therefore, crown the list of virtues mentioned in connection with the conflict between the flesh and the Spirit. If there is to be victory, it can only be as the Spirit of God enables a person to rule his own spirit.

In a day when violence, selfishness, apathy, and undisciplined living threaten to destroy our planet, it is imperative for Christians to set right examples. Our witness to the world must clearly note that the end of life is not duty but character. The Word of God is our best defense against becoming intemperate. Good preaching makes good disciples. Hiding God's Word in our hearts will keep us from sinning: "And take heed to yourselves, lest at any time your hearts be overcharged with surfeiting, and drunkenness, and cares of this life, and so that day come upon you unawares" (Luke 21:34). The disciplined Christian wins the prize and will take many others with him to glory!

CONCLUSION

The apostle Paul called our Christian experience a "walk," because it is similar to simply placing one foot before the other to reach our destination. In our daily walk, the Holy Spirit transforms our emotional lives, giving us love, joy, and peace. He strengthens our devotional lives, enabling us to perceive truth, read God's Word, pray, and trust God. The Holy Spirit also enables us to live victoriously, fostering our Christian growth, enabling us to witness, and empowering us for service. Such are true marks of a spiritual person and a spiritual church!

QUESTIONS

For Thought:

1. If we cannot teach spirituality as a subject or a skill, why do you think it is important to study this subject?
2. What do you think of the statement, "Every theology and every expression of spiritual life is imperfect, and we evangelicals are overdue for a dose of humility in this area."
3. In which areas of your experience do you need to see the fruit of temperance more?

For Discussion:

1. Discuss the difference in judging things and judging people. How do we measure our progress in this area?
2. Discuss the six inadequate patterns of spirituality and how they can be balanced.

3. List five ways an individual can promote the obvious bearing of the fruit of the Spirit in his or her life?

4. What is the importance of the three fruit of the Spirit that relate to our works of witness to the world and evangelism?

ACTIVITIES

1. On a scale of 1 to 5, rate the prominence of the nine fruit of the Spirit in your life.

2. Consider which two fruit of the Spirit need to be more evident in you.

3. Work on these things this week.

Chapter 13

THE HOLY SPIRIT AND
OUR DEVOTIONAL LIFE

Discuss the most difficult areas of having regular, personal devotions.

THE HOLY SPIRIT AND OUR DEVOTIONAL LIFE

by
Marcus V. Hand

Scripture: Jude 20

INTRODUCTION

All of life is itself devotional for the Christian. At all times and in every way believers seek to know God better and to worship Him. There is a personal discipline, however, in which we *purposefully* and *consciously* seek and worship Him. To be spiritually healthy, a Christian must develop and maintain what we call "a devotional life." The focus of this study is on how the Holy Spirit helps us in our pursuit of God and in our worship of Him.

At least three steps are involved in seeking and worshiping God: We must seek God in His Word, we must approach Him in prayer, and we must praise Him in worship. The Holy Spirit is "the One who is alongside" in each step, enhancing our personal perspectives with His wisdom, enriching our prayers in intercession, and intensifying our praise in worship!

THE SPIRIT ENHANCES PERSONAL PERSPECTIVES WITH HIS WISDOM (1 Corinthians 2:1-11)

The Holy Spirit makes the Word of God come alive for us. Martin

Niemöller, a German pastor, opposed Hitler during World War II and spent most of the war in German prison camps. Niemöller testified: "What did this book [the Bible] mean to me during the long and weary years of solitary confinement and then for the last four years at Dauchau? The Word of God was simply everything to me, comfort and strength, guidance and hope, master of my days and companion of my nights, the bread that kept me from starvation and the water of life that refreshed my soul."

When we read the Scripture, we are taught by the Spirit. He opens our minds to an understanding of the Word of God. Through the Spirit the Bible becomes the living Word of God for us. The Spirit enables us to understand reality. The Word takes on a new, fresh and glowing meaning. He opens the truth to our minds and hearts.

The Holy Spirit permits us to be privy to the mystery of God. "We speak wisdom among those who are mature, yet not the wisdom of this age, nor of the rulers of this age, who are coming to nothing. But we speak the wisdom of God in a mystery, the hidden wisdom which God ordained before the ages for our glory" (1 Corinthians 2:6, 7, *NKJV*).

The Greek word *musterion*, translated "mystery" here, does not mean a murky, complex message difficult to understand. An accurate synonym would be "secret." Barclay says it "means something whose meaning is hidden from those who have not been initiated, but crystal clear to those who have." It is understood as a secret message that is clear to those who have been informed, but puzzling to those who aren't in on it. The wisdom of God's message is hidden from those who do not believe.

This mystery of God's wisdom is spiritually understood. It is not discovered by intellectual activity. "God has revealed it to us by his Spirit" (v. 10).*

The Holy Spirit reveals to our understanding the meaning of events around us. The greatest event of history—the Crucifixion—took place in the generation in which Jesus lived. An unbelieving world could not understand the meaning of the Cross, however, because unbelievers had only intellectual comprehension of truths about Jesus. Paul said, "None of the rulers of this age understood it, for if they had, they would not have crucified the Lord of glory" (v. 8).

Spiritually enlightened and inspired, Paul understood and proclaimed the truth of the Gospel to all he met.

The Holy Spirit gives us insight and foresight into things the

world cannot comprehend. "As it is written: 'Eye has not seen, nor ear heard, nor have entered into the heart of man the things which God has prepared for those who love Him.' But God has revealed them to us through His Spirit. For the Spirit searches all things, yes, the deep things of God" (1 Corinthians 2:9, 10, *NKJV*).

In this passage, Paul was referring to Isaiah 64:4 where the Old Testament prophet points out that the enemies of God could never see, hear or comprehend what God was doing in the world. They still can't, Paul declares; these things are not known by empirical knowledge. *The Living Bible* describes it this way: "But we know about these things because God has sent his Spirit to tell us, and his Spirit searches out and shows us all of God's deepest secrets" (1 Corinthians 2:10).

The Holy Spirit teaches us the true meaning of intimacy with God. "Who among men knows the thoughts of a man except the man's spirit within him? In the same way no one knows the thoughts of God except the Spirit of God" (1 Corinthians 2:11). William Barclay comments on this passage in a very insightful way:

> Paul lays down that the only person who can tell us about God is the Spirit of God. He uses a human analogy. There are feelings so personal, things which are so private, experiences which are so intimate that no one knows them except a man's own spirit. Paul argues that the same is true of God. There are deep and intimate things in Him which only His Spirit knows; and that Spirit is the only Person who can lead us into really intimate knowledge of God.

One of the most meaningful works of the Holy Spirit is that in our devotional life, we can depend on God to give us wisdom—His wisdom! "If any of you lacks wisdom, let him ask of God, who gives to all liberally and without reproach, and it will be given to him" (James 1:5, *NKJV*). This promise does not relieve us of the human responsibility of learning all we can. A truly spiritual Christian is not intellectually lazy. Yet we know that the great discoveries of humanity have been revealed to us by God more than they have been discovered by our own efforts.

THE SPIRIT ENRICHES OUR PRAYERS WITH HIS INTERCESSION (Romans 8:5-27)

The child of God is blessed with two divine intercessors: Jesus and the Holy Spirit. Jesus intercedes for us in heaven (Romans 8:34). The

Holy Spirit prays for us and through us on earth (vv. 26, 27). As Dr. Ray H. Hughes writes, "The Spirit has channels to glory that human words cannot find unless touched by the power of God."

The Holy Spirit motivates us to pray. Romans 8 focuses on the work of the Spirit and how He leads us to a life of prayer. The exposition of this chapter unfolds in a meaningful way.

The Holy Spirit gives us a new mind-set. "Those who live according to the sinful nature have their minds set on what that nature desires; but those who live in accordance with the Spirit have their minds set on what the Spirit desires. The mind of sinful man is death, but the mind controlled by the Spirit is life and peace; the sinful mind is hostile to God. It does not submit to God's law, nor can it do so. Those controlled by the sinful nature cannot please God" (vv. 5-8).

The Holy Spirit gives us a new power of control. "You, however, are controlled not by the sinful nature but by the Spirit, if the Spirit of God lives in you. And if anyone does not have the Spirit of Christ, he does not belong to Christ" (v. 9).

The Holy Spirit gives us a new obligation. "Therefore, brothers, we have an obligation—but it is not to the sinful nature, to live according to it. For if you live according to the sinful nature, you will die; but if by the Spirit you put to death the misdeeds of the body, you will live" (vv. 12, 13).

The Holy Spirit gives us a new identity. "Because those who are led by the Spirit of God are sons of God. For you did not receive a spirit that makes you a slave again to fear, but you received the Spirit of sonship. And by him we cry, 'Abba, Father.' The Spirit himself testifies with our spirit that we are God's children" (vv. 14-16).

The Holy Spirit gives us new light on fallen creation. "The creation waits in eager expectation for the sons of God to be revealed. For the creation was subjected to frustration, not by its own choice, but by the will of the one who subjected it, in hope that the creation itself will be liberated from its bondage to decay and brought into the glorious freedom of the children of God" (vv. 19-21).

The animal world is violent. It is ruled by domination and fear—an unwritten law called the survival of the fittest. Nature's horrors include floods, hurricanes, droughts, tornadoes, earthquakes, typhoons, avalanches, and any number of other natural disasters. Humanity's pollution of the environment complicates an already volatile condition. No wonder creation groans, in Paul's analogy, like a woman in childbirth, awaiting deliverance.

The Holy Spirit gives us new hope in every situation. "We ourselves, who have the firstfruits of the Spirit, groan inwardly as we wait eagerly for our adoption as sons, the redemption of our bodies" (v. 23). Imperfections, liabilities, accidents, afflictions, and pain constantly remind us of our limitations. Disappointment, bereavement, and sorrow keep us earthbound. Wasted hours and neglected opportunities keep us tethered to this world.

So we groan. But we groan in expectancy. We know that one day we shall be with Christ (John 14:3). We know, too, that we shall be like Him (1 John 3:2). We know that we shall have glory with Him (Colossians 3:4). We know that this joy of being like Him and with Him will be a state that will last forever! When we groan within; we eagerly await the redemption of our bodies.

The Holy Spirit gives us new help in our praying. "In the same way, the Spirit helps us in our weakness. We do not know what we ought to pray for, but the Spirit himself intercedes for us with groans that words cannot express. And he who searches our hearts knows the mind of the Spirit, because the Spirit intercedes for the saints in accordance with God's will" (Romans 8:26, 27).

- The Holy Spirit prays for us and through us in our weakness.
- The Holy Spirit prays for us and through us when we don't know what to pray for.
- The Holy Spirit prays for us and through us when we cannot express ourselves in words.
- The Holy Spirit prays for us and through us, always, according to the will of God.

Praying in the Spirit puts one in direct communion with God, bypassing the mind. Paul prayed with his mind and with his spirit, in a known language and in an unknown language. Devotional tongues have value for the individual Christian's personal worship and prayer.

THE SPIRIT INTENSIFIES OUR PRAISE IN WORSHIP

"Enter into His gates with thanksgiving, and into His courts with praise. Be thankful to Him, and bless His name. For the Lord is good;

His mercy is everlasting, and His truth endures to all generations" (Psalm 100:4, 5, *NKJV*).

As we develop our devotional life, the Holy Spirit confirms God's presence in us. When we receive Christ into our hearts, we do it by faith. We live for Him by faith. Still, when we become His we do not live the life of faith without a witness. God provides an incomparable assurance: He gives the Holy Spirit to confirm His presence in us. "No one can say that Jesus is Lord except by the Holy Spirit" (1 Corinthians 12:3, *NKJV*). "By this we know that He abides in us, by the Spirit whom He has given us" (1 John 3:24, *NKJV*). Faith is sufficient, but faith isn't all. The reality of His Spirit in us confirms His presence.

As we develop our devotional life, the Holy Spirit endows us with spiritual gifts. "Gifts of the Spirit" is one of the church's most popular subjects. The meaning of the phrase, however, often varies with whoever uses it. The truth of Scripture is that all of us are gifted in some way; but we are gifted so that we can help others: "The manifestation of the Spirit is given to each one for the profit of all" (1 Corinthians 12:7, *NKJV*).

As we develop our devotional life, the Holy Spirit empowers us to give prophetic utterances and declarations of praise. "For they heard them speaking in tongues and praising God" (Acts 10:46). "Every day they continued to meet together . . . praising God and enjoying the favor of all the people" (2:46-47).

As we develop our devotional life, the Holy Spirit intensifies our personal worship and spiritual growth. "Be filled with the Spirit. Speak to one another with psalms, hymns and spiritual songs. Sing and make music in your heart to the Lord, always giving thanks to God the Father for everything, in the name of our Lord Jesus Christ. Submit to one another out of reverence for Christ" (Ephesians 5:18-21).

As we develop our devotional life, the Holy Spirit inspires personal, devotional singing. "If I pray in a tongue, my spirit prays. . . . What shall I do [then]? I will pray with my spirit, but I will also pray with my mind; *I will sing [praise] with my spirit, but I will also sing [praise] with my mind* " (1 Corinthians 14:14, 15).

As we develop our devotional life, the Holy Spirit intensifies our relationship with God and with each other. "In him you too are being built together to become a dwelling in which God lives by his Spirit"

(Ephesians 2:22). "Let the word of Christ dwell in you richly as you teach and admonish one another with all wisdom, and as you sing psalms, hymns and spiritual songs with gratitude in your hearts to God" (Colossians 3:16).

As we develop our devotional life, the Holy Spirit enables us to build ourselves up. "Build yourselves up in your most holy faith and pray in the Holy Spirit" (Jude 20). Through prayer, praise, singing, blessing, and thanksgiving we are drawn closer to God.

CONCLUSION

Paul is our example. He regularly practiced worship in the Spirit in his own private devotions. In 1 Corinthians 14, he referred to the private use of tongues directed to God. Verses 18 and 19 imply that Paul spoke in tongues more in private devotions than in public worship. He speaks with reverence and gratitude for the manifestations of the Holy Spirit which enabled him to pray, sing, praise and give thanks.

Let us thank God for the presence of the Holy Spirit in us. He is our helper, a comforting resource in our personal devotions.

*Scriptures are from the *New International Version* unless otherwise indicated.

QUESTIONS

For Thought:

1. Look closely at your personal devotional life. Make a list of things you can do to increase the quality of your private worship.
2. In what areas of your life have you found the truth of the concept: "The Holy Spirit gives us a new power of control."
3. In what four ways does the Holy Spirit help us in our praying?
4. In 1 Corinthians 14, Paul said the Holy Spirit enabled him to pray, sing, praise, and give thanks in worship. Have you found that the Spirit enables you in these area as well?

For Discussion:

1. Discuss the work of the two divine Intercessors: Jesus and the Holy Spirit.
2. Discuss the implications of the seven "new things" the Holy Spirit gives to us.
3. How does the Holy Spirit increase our praise in worship?

ACTIVITIES

Share with someone this week about an instance in which the Holy Spirit made a passage of Scripture come alive to you and helped you in a particular situation.

Chapter 1

NAMES OF THE HOLY SPIRIT
by
J. Anthony Lombard

Scripture: John 14:16

INTRODUCTION

There are distinct names for God and for Jesus Christ. The different names reveal the distinct personality and function of each member of the Godhead. The names of the Holy Spirit likewise reveal who He really is and how He works for us and in us.

SPIRIT OF GRACE (Hebrews 10:29)

  A. The Spirit of Grace reveals love's initiative.
  B. The Spirit of Grace reveals love's supremacy.
  C. The Spirit of Grace expresses God's love.

SPIRIT OF LIFE (Romans 8:2)

  A. The Spirit of Life deals with mankind in sin.
  B. The Spirit of Life deals with believers in hope.

SPIRIT OF ADOPTION (Romans 8:15)

  A. Adoption has to do with identity.
  B. Adoption has to do with authority.
  C. Adoption has to do with privileges.
  D. Adoption has to do with inheritance.

THE COMFORTER (John 14:16, 17)

  A. His ministry is the same as Jesus' in kind, but different in duration (John 14:16).

B. He gives validating witness of Jesus (John 15:26).

C. His ministry of fullness could not begin until Jesus' earthly ministry ended (John 16:7).

D. He will amplify truth and announce things to come (John 16:13).

CONCLUSION

The person and work of the Holy Spirit did not originate at Pentecost. The Holy Spirit's work began with Creation and continues today. We are witnesses to the mighty acts of the Spirit. More than a witness, however, He is an inner presence energizing and guiding us day by day. He speaks truth and gives comfort. He reveals Jesus and events to come.

Chapter 2

THE HOLY SPIRIT IN THE OLD TESTAMENT
by
Reginald W. Spooner

Scripture: Genesis 1:2

INTRODUCTION

Scripture introduces the Spirit in Genesis 1:1, 2. The Holy Spirit is always seen as moving. He is pro-active. He is Deity in motion. In fact the Holy Spirit is so active that He may be referred to as "the Restless One."

THE SPIRIT MOVED IN CREATION
(Genesis 1:1, 2; Isaiah 45:18; Genesis 6:3)

    A. His work in Genesis 1:1, 2

    B. A time lapse suggested

    C. The Spirit and light

THE SPIRIT MOVED IN HUMANITY
(Titus 3:5; John 3:8; Genesis 4:26; Acts 2:2; Psalm 139:7-12)

    A. The breath of God

    B. The wind of God

THE SPIRIT MOVED IN GOVERNMENTS
(Numbers 11:16, 17, 24-26; 1 Samuel 10:12; 2 Samuel 23:2)

    A. National leaders

    B. King Saul

    C. King David

THE SPIRIT MOVED ON THE PROPHETS (Nehemiah 9:30; 2 Peter 1:21; Isaiah 8:11; Malachi 4; Matthew 11:13, 14)

A. Concerning Israel in Nehemiah 9:30

B. Concerning the Word of God in 2 Peter 1:21

C. Concerning specific messages in Isaiah 8:11

D. Concerning Jesus in Malachi 4; Matthew 11:13, 14

THE SPIRIT MOVED IN PEACEFUL WAYS (Numbers 9:15-23; Psalm 91:1; 2 Corinthians 13:14; Ephesians 2:22)

A. The Restless One rested

B. The cloud in the wilderness

C. The communion of the Holy Ghost

D. Shut in with God

CONCLUSION

The image of the dove that Noah released, returning with a green leaf in its beak, symbolizes the new beginning of the Holy Spirit. He is always interested in new beginnings. He has staked out a claim on us, and He is ever at cross-purposes with the world.

You and I must move with the moving Holy Spirit. As the cloud lifts, we say with Moses that its time to move again: "Rise up, Lord, and let thine enemies be scattered" (Numbers 10:35).

Chapter 3

SYMBOLS OF THE HOLY SPIRIT
by
Homer G. Rhea

Scripture: Luke 3:22

INTRODUCTION

Our understanding of the person and work of the Holy Spirit should be enhanced through a study of the symbols of the Holy Spirit.

FIRE

A. John contrasted the baptisms he and Jesus offered.

B. The believers saw tongues of what looked like fire.

C. The fire symbolized the divine presence.

D. To be filled with the Spirit is to be brought completely under His control.

WIND

A. Ezekiel prophesied to the wind.

B. Ezekiel's prophecy referred to the whole house of Israel.

C. Believers in the Upper Room heard a sound from heaven as of the blowing of a violent wind.

D. The wind symbolized the life-giving, energizing power of the Spirit.

WATER

A. Jesus extended an invitation to thirsty souls to come to Him to have their thirst quenched.

B. The believer who drinks of this living water becomes himself a fountain for others.

C. Jesus had the Holy Spirit in mind when He spoke of quenching spiritual thirst.

D. Water symbolized the effectiveness and sufficiency of the Spirit's ministry.

DOVE

A. When Jesus expressed His desire to be baptized by John, John protested strenuously.

B. By His baptism in water, Jesus identified Himself with the work of redemption.

C. The Spirit of God descended in the form of a dove and rested upon Jesus.

D. The dove symbolized the purity, innocence, meekness, and graciousness of the Spirit.

SEAL

A. A seal is a mark of ownership.

B. The Holy Spirit puts His stamp upon the heart.

C. This divine seal comes from God to those who are in Christ.

D. The seal symbolized the importance of the role of the Spirit in redemption.

OIL

A. Samuel poured a flask of oil on Saul's head, anointing him to be leader over Israel.

B. When Samuel anointed David, the Spirit of the Lord came upon him in power.

C. Our success comes not by might, nor by power, but by the Spirit of God.

D. Oil symbolized the need for the power of the Holy Spirit in the fulfillment of God's work.

CONCLUSION

The various functions of the person and work of the Holy Spirit are made clearer by considering the Biblical symbols of the Spirit.

Chapter 4

THE HOLY SPIRIT AND CHRISTIAN LIVING
by
Mark L. Williams

Scripture: John 16:8-11

INTRODUCTION

Without a doubt the 20th century will be remembered in Christendom as a century of the Spirit. Perhaps at no other time in human history has the church of the Lord Jesus Christ witnessed such a visible, global inbreaking of the Holy Spirit's power. However, while we celebrate the visible manifestations of power, we tend to overlook the practical impact of the Holy Spirit on daily living. The mighty demonstrations of power are not an end in themselves but a means to an end, that is, that men and women might be saved and live the Christlife.

THE IDENTITY OF THE HOLY SPIRIT

A. The Holy Spirit is God.
  1. His divinity is set forth by the position in which He is placed in the Holy Trinity (2 Corinthians 13:14; Matthew 28:19; Acts 5:4).
  2. His divinity is established by the attributes He possesses.
    a. The Holy Spirit is omniscient (Isaiah 11:2; 1 Corinthians 2:9-12; John 14:26; 16:13).
    b. The Holy Spirit is omnipresent (Psalm 139:7; Hebrews 9:14; John 14:26).
    c. The Holy Spirit is omnipotent (Luke 1:37).
B. The Holy Spirit is a divine person.
  1. He possesses the characteristics of mind (Romans 8:27), will

(1 Corinthians 12:11), understanding (2:10, 11), and emotion (Ephesians 4:30).

2. He engages in activities such as speaking (Revelation 2:7), interceding (Romans 8:26), teaching (John 14:26), commanding (Acts 16:6, 7), appointing (20:28), testifying (John 15:26), and leading (16:13).

3. He can be grieved (Ephesians 4:30); He can be lied to (Acts 5:3); He can be insulted (Hebrews 10:29); He can be blasphemed (Matthew 12:31, 32).

THE HOLY SPIRIT IN REGENERATION

A. The Holy Spirit convicts of sin (John 16:7-11).
B. The Holy Spirit is the agent for the new birth.
1. We are born of the Spirit (John 3:5, 8).
2. We are baptized into Christ by the Spirit (1 Corinthians 12:13).
3. The Holy Spirit identifies us as children of God (1 John 4:13; Romans 8:9, 14-16).
C. The Holy Spirit seals us (Ephesians 1:13, 14).

THE INDWELLING OF THE HOLY SPIRIT

A. We are temples of the Holy Spirit (1 Corinthians 3:16; 6:19; Romans 8:11).
B. This is a sobering responsibility (1 Corinthians 6:18; Colossians 3:5, 8-10; 2 Corinthians 6:14—7:1).

CONCLUSION

The Holy Spirit regenerates us, dwells within us, and enables us to live clean in a dirty place!

Chapter 5

BAPTISM IN THE HOLY SPIRIT
by
Sam McGraner

Scripture: Acts 2:1–4

INTRODUCTION

The vision given to the prophet Joel in the Old Testament is today an experience people receive in every corner of the world. The baptism in the Holy Spirit is real and verifiable. Of paramount importance is the fact that this blessing is available to believers today. It is the will of God that the church be a Spirit-led, Spirit-filled body. The baptism in the Holy Spirit should be the rule, not the exception. This experience is for you!

THE PROMISE

A. Joel was familiar with the Spirit's coming upon select men, like Samson and David, in the Old Testament.

B. Joel foresaw the day when the Holy Spirit would be poured out on all flesh.

C. As the time for the fulfillment of Joel's prophecy drew near, God renewed the promise through the words of John the Baptist and Jesus.

THE FULFILLMENT

A. The outpouring of the Holy Spirit on the Day of Pentecost is second in importance only to the birth, death, and resurrection of Jesus.

B. Several Biblical precedents were set in the outpouring of the Spirit—precedents that are valid today.

C. Peter's anointed message on the Day of Pentecost boldly declared that Joel's prophecy was fulfilled in himself and those with him.

THE EXPERIENCE

A. The baptism in the Holy Spirit is an intensely personal experience.
B. The baptism in the Holy Spirit will follow Biblical precedents.
C. The baptism in the Holy Spirit is a daily walk that is renewed in times of worship or personal devotion.

THE SCOPE

A. With the baptism in the Holy Spirit comes the power to witness.
B. Wherever the witness of Jesus Christ is given, the opportunity to receive the baptism in the Holy Spirit is available.
C. The Holy Spirit baptism is available to "the ends of the earth" (Acts 1:8, *NIV*), and to "all whom the Lord our God will call" (2:39, *NIV*).

CONCLUSION

The baptism in the Holy Spirit is not an exclusive blessing for the elite or a reward for the pious. It is a gift for everyone who believes. It empowers us for service and ignites our testimony. It makes us better people, better Christians, and better workers for Christ.

You need this experience. It is for you.

Chapter 6

POWER FOR SERVICE

by
Gerald J. Johnson

Scripture: Luke 24:49

INTRODUCTION

Power for service resides in the baptism in the Holy Spirit. Spirit-baptized believers obey God by sharing in His work. Consequently, His divine power is released in service. Divine energy becomes effective when it is used for the purpose for which it is directed. Faith and obedience release this divine power in active energy toward human need. The Word of God gives hundreds of assurances of the Holy Spirit's empowering presence to ensure effective service.

JESUS PROMISED SUPERNATURAL POWER (Luke 24:49; Acts 1:8)

A. The Holy Spirit invites—He is with us (John 14:17).
B. The Holy Spirit indwells—He is in us (Romans 8:9).
C. The Holy Spirit infills—He comes upon us (Acts 1:8; Hebrews 2:3, 4).

JESUS SENT THE HOLY SPIRIT (Acts 2:1-4)

A. There was a supernatural sequence initiated on the Day of Pentecost.
B. The prophecy of Joel 2:28, "On all flesh," was fulfilled.

BELIEVERS MINISTERED IN THE POWER OF THE SPIRIT (Acts 2:14-18)

A. The apostles witnessed with great power.

1. The Spirit-baptized believers ministered through the power of *agape* love.

2. The Spirit-baptized believers received power to think Christ's thoughts, live Christ's life, and work Christ's works.

3. Peter's service is recorded before and after the Holy Spirit baptism.

B. A new era began at Pentecost.

1. The Holy Spirit urged the apostles and believers to carry out their witness to the world.

2. Paul's farewell at Ephesus recounts service empowered by the Spirit (Acts 20:16-38).

POST-APOSTOLIC MINISTRY AND BEYOND (Acts 2:39)

A. Laypeople carried out the Great Commission for the first three centuries.

1. The state took on the responsibility of making its people Christian.

2. The Reformation sparked some soulwinning service.

3. The Catholic Counter-Reformation gave the Roman Catholic version of Christianity.

B. God has given us the task of serving and winning our generation.

1. Power for service is the experience of a Christ-filled spirit.

2. Power for service is the expression of a Christ-centered heart.

3. Power for service is the extension of a Christ-mastered will.

SUPERNATURAL SPIRITUAL POWER FOR SERVICE TODAY (2 Timothy 3:16, 17)

A. Apologetic: God's Word and Holy Spirit baptism today

1. God's Word authenticates His power for service today.

2. God's Word authorizes His power for service today.

3. God's Word applies His power for service today.

B. Spirit-baptism and Christ's return are linked for powerful service.
   1. The Holy Spirit prompts prophetic service (Acts 2:14-21).
   2. The Holy Spirit prompts powerful service (2 Corinthians 4:7).
   3. The Holy Spirit prompts practical service (1 Corinthians 1:26-31).
   4. The Holy Spirit prompts personal ambassador service (2 Corinthians 5:20).

CONCLUSION (2 Peter 3:9)

Attention, all Spirit-baptized believers: Are you witnessing to the lost as God's anointed ambassador? If not you, *who*? If not here, *where*? If not now, *when*? "Behold, He cometh!"

Chapter 7

GIFTS OF THE HOLY SPIRIT
by
Paul O. Lombard Jr.

SCRIPTURE: 1 Corinthians 12:1-31

INTRODUCTION

Gift-giving is a practice that occurs all through our lives. We give and receive gifts on many different occasions. Likewise, God also gives gifts: "Every good gift and every perfect gift . . . cometh down from the Father" (James 1:17). God's gifts are both unique and costly—His Son and the baptism in the Holy Spirit. Furthermore, the baptism in the Holy Spirit is the prerequisite for receiving spiritual gifts.

SPIRITUAL GIFTS TESTIFY (vv. 1-3)

A. There is a difference between "Gift of the Holy Spirit" and "Gifts of the Spirit."

B. Knowledge testifies.
   1. The tenacity and ferocity of demonic power
   2. The power and authority of God
   3. Armor provides defense; gifts provide offense.
   4. God speaks in both the old and new covenants.

C. Emotionalism is a factor.
   1. Heathenism is emotional.
   2. Christianity is based on a confession.
   3. A spiritual gift passes the doctrinal test of truth.

SPIRITUAL GIFTS EDIFY (vv. 4-11)

A. Diversity
   1. Variety brings life.
   2. "Diversities" but "the same"
B. Natural ability versus anointing
   1. Natural abilities are inherent.
   2. Anointed abilities are Spirit-given.
C. Authority and miracles
   1. The church is to minister in power and authority.
   2. Common faith is not equal with the gift of faith.
D. The prophetic voice
   1. God uses men and women to give prophetic utterances.
   2. God forbids communication with works of darkness.

SPIRITUAL GIFTS UNIFY (vv. 12-31)

A. Unity and the human body
   1. The body depends on functioning members.
   2. The Spirit is one, but the ministries are many.
B. Unity and the Spirit
   1. Two measures of water: baptism and a drink
   2. The sovereignty of God
C. Unity, not uniformity
   1. Unity is not sameness.
   2. The unity of power quickly adds up.

CONCLUSION

For every kind of work the church must do, God has supplied a corresponding gift. There is an infrastructure of gifts, helps, and government which ensures that the church will not fail for lack of power.

Chapter 8

MINISTRY GIFTS

by
Lane Lavender

Scripture: Romans 12:6-18

INTRODUCTION

All of the gifts of the Spirit are needed in the church today, especially ministry gifts which are needed to keep a church going and growing. The New Testament gives lists of spiritual gifts: Romans 12:3-8; 1 Corinthians 12:8-10, 28-30; Ephesians 4:11. Ministry gifts are the special graces expressed specifically for the edification, exhortation, and unity of the body of Christ and its outreach. Those who exercise these gifts must reflect the character of Christ for the gifts to be effective.

A BIBLICAL VIEW OF MINISTRY GIFTS

   A. Prophecy

      1. This gift refers to foretelling as well as forthtelling (1 Corinthians 14:1, 3).

      2. A message of prophecy is directed to the church, but may affect sinners (1 Corinthians 14:3, 4, 22, 24, 25).

      3. The gift should always correspond to the faith of the prophet (Romans 12:6).

   B. Serving (ministry, helps)

      1. This gift usually referred to the work of deacons in the New Testament; their ministry included monitoring the money and overseeing the ministry to the widows, the poor, and the sick (Acts 6:2-4).

      2. Servant leadership is a Scriptural requirement for those who lead our churches and ministries (Isaiah 66:2; Matthew 20:20-28).

C. Teaching

      1. There is a difference between gifted teachers and teachers with "the gift." Those with the gift of teaching have a supernatural ability to communicate the truth of God's Word to people's lives with the anointing of God.

      2. The Holy Spirit is our teacher (John 6:45; 14:17, 26; 2 Corinthians 3:3), but God also expects us to be good students of His Word.

D. Exhorting (encouraging)

      1. The exhorter is used of the Spirit to encourage, motivate, comfort, and give direction to the body of Christ.

      2. The Holy Spirit is the great Comforter and He knows how to minister to our needs (John 14:16).

E. Giving

      1. The gift of giving relates to sharing material aid with those in need.

      2. Each of the Scriptural examples of the gift of giving come immediately following an outpouring of the Holy Spirit (Acts 2:44, 45; 4:34-37).

      3. This gift is not limited to the wealthy (Ephesians 4:28).

F. Leadership (ruling, governing)

      1. This gift has to do with the oversight of something.

      2. It must be operated with humility and servanthood to be valid.

G. Acts of Mercy (showing mercy)

      1. This gift concerns the personal care of the needy, the sick, the hungry, the prisoners, and those needing clothes.

      2. A good Scriptural example of this gift is Dorcas (Acts 9:36-39).

A BIBLICAL ATTITUDE TOWARD MINISTRY GIFTS

A. Love (Romans 12:9, 10; 1 Corinthians 14:1)

B. Unity (1 Corinthians 12:12-26)

C. Humility (Romans 12:16)

CONCLUSION

Churches that don't operate in the gifts of the Spirit are like automobiles without engines—they run on human effort. God has a greater potential in store for the church and the believer. He has given the church the ministry gifts to help us fulfill our potential for Christ's kingdom through the supernatural power of His Spirit (Ephesians 3:20).

Chapter 9

THE HOLY SPIRIT AND DISCIPLESHIP

by
Daniel L. Black

SCRIPTURE: Luke 14:25-27

INTRODUCTION

Christian discipleship requires a level of commitment to Jesus Christ that we are not capable of giving by our strength alone. To be disciples of Jesus, we must submit to the sanctifying work of the Holy Spirit, the teaching of the Holy Spirit, and the guidance of the Holy Spirit.

DISCIPLESHIP AND SANCTIFICATION BY THE HOLY SPIRIT

A. We need sanctification for discipleship.

B. Obedience to Christ is doing and being.

C. Sanctification is for obedience to Christ.

D. Real discipleship is holy living.

E. Devotion to Christ must be the same as that given to God.

DISCIPLESHIP AND THE TEACHING OF THE HOLY SPIRIT

A. We need the teaching of the Spirit for discipleship.

B. Jesus was a teacher.

C. There can be no discipleship without teaching and learning.

D. There is a spiritual dimension to being a disciple of Christ.

E. The Holy Spirit enlightens and convinces by teaching.

F. The Holy Spirit is a teacher like Jesus.

DISCIPLESHIP AND THE GUIDANCE OF THE HOLY SPIRIT

    A. We need the guidance of the Spirit for discipleship.

    B. There are distinctions between the general and particular calls to discipleship.

    C. The Spirit guides in the general call to discipleship.

    D. The Spirit guides in particular calls to discipleship.

CONCLUSION

If I am willing to be a disciple of Jesus Christ, the Holy Spirit is able to make me a disciple. Through sanctification He will bring me into obedience to Christ. He will teach me how to give my soul, my life, my all to Christ. He will guide me in the way of truth to the complete fulfillment of my calling to Christian discipleship. Am I willing to submit to the Spirit?

Chapter 10

THE HOLY SPIRIT AND EVANGELISM
by
James E. Cossey

SCRIPTURE: Acts 9:1-22; 13:1-12

INTRODUCTION

An ailing Billy Graham was released from the hospital at age 77, and was asked about his future plans. "I plan to continue to preach the gospel!" he replied. "I have several more good years to give to the ministry."

Evangelism is the heartbeat of God. John 3:16 tells us that God sent His only begotten Son as an evangelist. Tradition calls John the beloved disciple, "the evangelist." Without doubt, those who have most profoundly affected the Christian faith through the centuries were Jesus himself, the apostle Peter, John, and Paul.

CHOSEN TO EVANGELIZE

A. The greatest evangelist of all time was perhaps the apostle Paul.
   1. It wasn't just a career choice; it was more than a chosen vocation.
   2. Paul never planned such a life. His plans were changed because he was literally arrested by the Holy Spirit, and chosen.
   3. Saul of Tarsus, as he was known, was on a mission of murder, but he met Jesus who was on a mission of mercy. The dispenser of death met the Giver of life.

B. Discipleship is a public commitment.
   1. It was important for Saul to acknowledge Christ publicly.
   2. Those he had persecuted needed to know of his conversion (Acts 9:13, 14).
   3. It was necessary for the church to acknowledge or affirm Saul's experience with Christ (Acts 9:15).
C. The beauty of evangelism is that God doesn't see us as we are.
   1. Sauls are all around us!
   2. No obvious potential for good can be seen in their lives.
   3. But Jesus loves them—not their values, lifestyle, or vocabulary—and He seeks them.

FILLED WITH POWER (Acts 9:17-19)

A. An enabling for engagement
   1. It is one thing to be chosen to evangelize, and something else to be anointed for the task.
   2. The anointing makes the difference.
B. An anointing with authority
   1. The anointing gave Paul authority.
   2. The anointing will give us authority.
C. An unction for usefulness
   1. The unction is the anointing (1 John 2:20).
   2. You know when it's missing.
   3. It is a gift from God.

WITNESSING IN POWER (Acts 9:20-22; 13:1-12)

A. Expressive power
B. Progressive power
C. Impressive power

CONCLUSION

Sometimes we miss the mark. The great need of the hour is for the preaching of the Word of God. But the greatest witness is the believer who mirrors the Christlife every day! The greatest preacher or teacher is the one who walks what he talks. The greatest evangelist is the one who can meet the devil on his own territory, stare him in the eye, and tell it like it is.

Chapter 11

WORSHIPING IN SPIRIT AND TRUTH
by
Samuel D. Adkerson

Scripture: Acts 2:42-47

INTRODUCTION

God has created each individual with the capacity to worship. Ancient man instinctively reached to embrace an authority, a power, or a person beyond himself. Men today still have their gods. But the only true Deity, the only One worthy of our worship, is Jehovah God who exists in the Father, Son, and Holy Spirit.

THE COMPONENTS OF CORPORATE WORSHIP

A. The altar
1. Spiritual problems are solved at the altar.
2. Physical miracles take place at the altar.
3. Psychological and emotional problems are solved there.
4. Social problems are solved by the God who heals.

B. The Sacraments
1. The Lord's Supper
2. Washing the saints' feet
3. Water baptism

THE ELEMENTS OF CORPORATE WORSHIP

A. Tithes and offerings
B. Prayer
C. Joy and praise

SOME GIFTS FOR CORPORATE WORSHIP

   A. Motivational Gifts (Romans 12:6-8)
      1. Prophecy
      2. Service (ministry)
      3. Teaching
      4. Exhortation
      5. Giving
      6. Leadership
      7. Mercy
   B. Ministry Gifts (1 Corinthians 12:8-10, 28; Ephesians 4:11; 1 Peter 4:9)
      1. Wisdom
      2. Faith
      3. Knowledge
      4. Miracles
      5. Discernment
      6. Tongues
      7. Interpretation
      8. Apostleship
      9. Healing
     10. Helps
     11. Evangelism
     12. Pastoring
     13. Hospitality

THE UNITY OF CORPORATE WORSHIP

THE RESULTS OF CORPORATE WORSHIP

   A. In the altar
      1. What the altar invitation should not do
      2. What the altar invitation should do
   B. In the community
      1. Reverential trust
      2. Praise and thanksgiving
      3. Willingness to share

CONCLUSION

What gifts and ministries are available to enhance the contemporary witness? When the elements, the components, the gifts, and the unity are all properly in place for God's people, true spiritual worship results. Worship then becomes a privilege rather than a program to be conducted. It is a joy rather than a religious "jangling." Such worship is truly experienced in spirit and in truth. It glorifies and honors God, while uplifting and strengthening the worshipers.

Chapter 12

THE SPIRITUAL CHURCH
by
T. David Sustar

SCRIPTURE: Galatians 5:22-26

INTRODUCTION

What is the criteria by which we judge spirituality? The Scriptures reveal two important items: "But the natural man receiveth not the things of the Spirit of God: for they are foolishness unto him: neither can he know them, because they are spiritually discerned. But he that is spiritual judgeth all things, yet he himself is judged of no man" (1 Corinthians 2:14-15). It seems that we judge "things" but not one another (Matthew 7:1).

The second insight is that spiritual things are taught (spiritually discerned) by the Spirit himself. This means that we cannot teach spirituality as a subject, like Old Testament, or as a skill, like preaching. Spirituality must be a part of our being, or it is nothing at all. It is keeping in step with the Spirit (Galatians 5:25).

THE BIBLICAL VIEW OF SPIRITUALITY

    A. The greatest commandment instructs us regarding spirituality.
        1. Total devotion to God
        2. Expressed in love of neighbor (Mark 12:28-34; Luke 10:25-37)
    B. There are inadequate patterns of spirituality.
        1. Legalistic pattern
        2. Libertine pattern
        3. Self-denigrating pattern
        4. Self-affirming pattern

5. Privation pattern
6. Wealth pattern

C. We are each His "workmanship" (Ephesians 2:10) and cannot be copies of one another.

BEING BEFORE DOING

A. God is more concerned about what we are *being* than what we are *doing*.
   1. Spirit-empowered service begins with a clean heart.
   2. Personal holiness commits believers to Christ's mission in the world, and holy love motivates them to joyful, effective service.

B. Paul believed *faith, hope,* and *love* were the critical elements by which a spiritual individual and church would be known.

C. Paul enlarged his list in Galatians 5:22 to include nine fruit of the Spirit.

IN FELLOWSHIP WITH GOD (LOVE, JOY, PEACE)

A. Love is the foundation and peak of the Christian experience.
   1. Love is based on a relationship with God and is borne out in our relationship with others.
   2. Love is "shed abroad in our hearts by the Holy Ghost" (Romans 5:5).

B. Joy is not so much the pleasure of doing but of being.
   1. Joy is a gift of grace.
   2. Joy illuminates all the Christian virtues.

C. Peace is the condition of freedom from strife internally and externally.
   1. Peace is a Biblical command: "Have peace one with another" (Mark 9:50).
   2. Peace is a work of the Holy Ghost (John 14:26, 27).
   3. Peace is to be resident in all the churches (1 Corinthians 14:33).

IN HARMONY WITH ONE ANOTHER (PATIENCE, GENTLENESS, GOODNESS)

A. Patience is steadfastness in obedience to God despite pressures to deny Him.

1. Circumstances and people test our patience.

2. Any person full of the Spirit will be a patient person (Ephesians 4:2).

B. Gentleness is kindness in dealing with our fellowman.

1. Our ministry must have tenderness and gentleness.

2. Gentleness is one of the greatest needs of the church today.

C. Goodness has to do with love in action.

1. Goodness is generous giving.

2. Goodness is righteousness demonstrated in everyday living.

IN WITNESS TO THE WORLD (FAITHFULNESS, MEEKNESS, TEMPERANCE)

A. "Faithfulness" is a correct rendering of the word *faith*.

1. Our blessed hope lies in the reliability of God.

2. This faith is firmly founded in the Word of God.

B. Meekness has nothing to do with weakness.

1. Meekness is power in submission, strength under control, authority under discipline.

2. Meekness will bring the promise of God to pass (2 Chronicles 7:14).

C. Temperance is self-control, the victory over desire.

1. The Spirit helps us rule our own spirit.

2. In a day when violence, selfishness, apathy, and undisciplined living threaten to destroy our planet, it is imperative that Christians set the right example.

CONCLUSION

If our daily walk reveals the fruit of the Spirit, a desire for the Word, prayer, and a trust in God, we will show the world the true marks of a spiritual person and church!

Chapter 13

THE HOLY SPIRIT AND OUR DEVOTIONAL LIFE

by
Marcus V. Hand

SCRIPTURE: Jude 20

INTRODUCTION

All of life is itself devotional for the Christian. There is a personal discipline, however, in which we purposefully and consciously seek and worship Him. In fact, to be spiritually healthy, a Christian must develop and maintain his devotional life. The Holy Spirit helps the Spirit-filled believer to do so by being his all-sufficient resource.

THE HOLY SPIRIT ENHANCES OUR PERSONAL PERSPECTIVES WITH HIS HIDDEN WISDOM (1 Corinthians 2:1-11).

    A. The Holy Spirit makes the Word of God come alive for us (vv. 1-5).

    B. The Holy Spirit makes us privy to the mystery of God (vv. 6, 7).

    C. The Holy Spirit reveals to our understanding the meaning of events around us (v. 8).

    D. The Holy Spirit gives us insight and foresight into things the world cannot comprehend (vv. 9, 10).

    E. The Holy spirit teaches us the true meaning of intimacy with God (v. 11).

THE HOLY SPIRIT ENRICHES OUR PRAYERS WITH HIS INTERCESSION (Romans 8:5-27).

    A. The Holy Spirit gives us a new mind-set (vv. 5-8).

B. The Holy Spirit gives us a new power of control (v. 9).

C. The Holy Spirit gives us a new obligation (vv. 12, 13).

D. The Holy Spirit gives us a new identity (vv. 14-16).

E. The Holy Spirit gives us new light on fallen creation (vv. 19-21).

F. The Holy Spirit gives us new hope in our situation (v. 23).

G. The Holy Spirit gives us new help in our praying (vv. 26, 27).

   1. The Holy Spirit prays for us and through us in our weakness.

   2. The Holy Spirit prays for us and through us when we don't know what to pray for.

   3. The Holy Spirit prays for us and through us when we cannot express ourselves in words.

THE HOLY SPIRIT INTENSIFIES OUR PRAISE IN WORSHIP

A. As we develop our devotional life, the Holy Spirit confirms God's presence in us (1 Corinthians 12:3; 1 John 3:24).

B. As we develop our devotional life, the Holy Spirit endows us with spiritual gifts (1 Corinthians 12:7).

C. As we develop our devotional life, the Holy Spirit empowers us to give prophetic utterances and declarations of praise (Acts 2:46, 47; 10:46).

D. As we develop our devotional life, the Holy Spirit intensifies our personal worship and spiritual growth (Ephesians 5:18-21).

E. As we develop our devotional life, the Holy Spirit inspires personal, devotional singing (1 Corinthians 14:14, 15).

F. As we develop our devotional life, the Holy Spirit intensifies our relationship with God and with each other (Ephesians 2:22; Colossians 3:16).

G. As we develop our devotional life, the Holy Spirit enables us to build ourselves up (Jude 20).

CONCLUSION

Paul depended on the Holy Spirit in his devotional life. He set an example for us (1 Corinthians 14).

ABOUT THE WRITERS

ABOUT THE WRITERS

Homer G. Rhea, L.H.D., editor in chief of Church of God publications, lives in Cleveland, Tennessee. He is the author of *A New Creation: A Study in Salvation* and *Come, Worship With Us.* A popular speaker, he is also the compiler of *The Pentecostal Minister Sermon Resource Manual,* Volumes 4 and 5, as well as this study. He serves as first vice president of the International Pentecostal Press Association; president of the International Pentecostal Press Association, North American Chapter; and as vice president of the Pentecostal/Charismatic Christian Education Alliance.

Samuel D. Adkerson, senior pastor of Broadmoor Church of God, lives in Nashville, Tennessee. He has served his denomination as evangelist, pastor, state director of youth and Christian education, and state evangelism director. A well-known writer, he was educated at Middle Tennessee State University and Clarksville School of Theology.

Daniel L. Black, Th.D., editor-writer of adult Sunday school curriculum at Pathway Press, lives in Cleveland, Tennessee. A former pastor and a respected Bible teacher, Dr. Black has served his denomination in several capacities. He holds degrees from Ridgedale Theological Seminary and Clarksville School of Theology. He is the author of two books: *Never a Day Too Much* and *A Layman's Guide to the Holy Spirit.*

James E. Cossey, Th.D., senior pastor of Loxley Church of God, lives in Loxley Alabama. He has served as pastor, state director of youth and Christian education, and editor of missions publications. He was educated at Luther Rice Seminary and Clarksville School of Theology. He has had many articles published in denominational publications.

Marcus V. Hand, editorial assistant at Pathway Press, lives in Cleveland, Tennessee. Educated at the University of Georgia and the Church of God School of Theology, he has served as a pastor, evangelist, and editor of various denominational magazines. He is the author of *Put Your Arms Around the World, I Saw a Vision, Reaching People, Linked Lives, A Potpourri of Pentecostal Preaching* (compiler and editor), and *Turning Point* (with Lee Savage).

Gerald J. Johnson Sr., D.Min., is senior pastor of the Providence Church of God and lives in Mobile, Alabama. A prominent evangelist, pastor, and church planter, he is often asked to speak on college campuses and on Christian television. He was educated at Lee College, Assembly of God Theological Seminary, and Bethany Theological Seminary. His writings appear in Church of God periodicals and manuals on evangelism and pastoral ministry.

A. Lane Lavender, senior pastor of Harvest Worship Center, lives in Lexington, Kentucky. He has served as a youth pastor and as a state director of youth and Christian education. A popular speaker, he has been featured in camp meetings, youth camps, and retreats. He is a graduate of the Church of God School of Theology. His writings are often seen in Church of God publications.

J. Anthony Lombard, curriculum sales coordinator for Pathway Press, lives in Ringgold, Georgia. He has served as a pastor and as state director of youth and Christian education. He was educated at Lee College and the Church of God School of Theology. His writings appear often in Church of God publications.

Paul Lombard Jr., senior pastor of College Park Church of God, lives in Huntsville, Alabama. He has served his denomination as district overseer and a member of the Alabama State Council. He was educated at the Church of God School of Theology. The writer is serving as adjunct professor of Lee College and has been a visiting professor at Korean Bible College in Seoul Korea.

Sam McGraner is senior pastor of Family Ministries Center in Sidney, Ohio. In addition to serving as an evangelist and a pastor, he has been a denominational administrator, serving as a state director of youth and Christian education. He was educated at Lee College, and his writings are frequently published in Church of God publications.

Reginald W. Spooner, Th.D., founder and president of Vessel Christian College and Bible School, lives in Port St. Lucie, Florida. He was educated at Lee College and Logos Christian College. A pastor for many years, he is now engaged in training younger men and women for ministry. He is the author of *Eighteen Ways to Healing* and *The Truth About Prosperity.*

T. David Sustar, president of East Coast Bible College, lives in Charlotte, North Carolina. An accomplished administrator, he has served as pastor, district overseer, state director of youth and Christian education, and international director of youth and Christian education. He is the author of *Youth and World Missions, Witnessing to Jehovah's Witnesses, A Layman's Guide to the Fruit of the Spirit, A Sure Foundation*, and *Transforming Faith: Reproducing the Christlife.*

Mark L. Williams, senior pastor of the South Cleveland Church of God, lives in Cleveland, Tennessee. A noted evangelist, conference and camp meeting speaker, he is often invited to speak on college campuses and is widely featured in citywide evangelistic crusades. He was educated at the Church of God School of Theology.